Kendall Hunt
publishing company

Doing the

TRANSCULTURAL THING

EDITED BY
Michael **SCHWARTZ**

Explorations in Living in the United States

Kendall Hunt
publishing company

www.kendallhunt.com
Send all inquiries to:
4050 Westmark Drive
Dubuque, IA 52004-1840

Copyright © 2015 by Michael W. Schwartz

ISBN 978-1-4652-7034-4

Contents

Introduction

So, why a book on culture and what is transculture? Clair Kramsch (1998) identifies three characteristics that link language and culture: "language expresses cultural identity; language embodies cultural identity; language symbolizes cultural identity" (p. 3). Culture is also a phenomenon that is expressed through shared community practices; thus, culture, language, and community are inextricably linked. Whether we are aware of it or not, every utterance we produce is an expression of who we are as individuals and what we believe. So when we begin the process of learning an additional language, we are not only learning a new linguistic code (basic vocabulary and structures) that allow us to ask for directions, to shop for clothes, or to interact with a teacher, we are having to relearn how to be.

> In language learning, interpreting and creating meanings involves an intercultural act of decentering as learners examine phenomena and experience their own cultural situatedness while seeking to enter into the culture worlds of others. It requires an act of engagement in which learners compare their own cultural assumptions, expectations, practices, and meanings with those of others, recognizing that these are formed within a cultural context that is different from their own (Scarino 2014, 391).

In other words, we struggle to find the same words that we would use to express, embody, and symbolize our cultural identity in the new language. In this way, we embark on a transient journey from culture 1 to culture 2 or 3, where we interact not only the lexicon and grammar of the new language but a new way of thinking and perceiving the world. In this process a part of our identity ventures into and out of, straddling at times, multiple cultures. It is this fluid and unstable process of moving to and from, and between cultures that I conceptualize as transculture.

The units in this book cover topics familiar to people from all over the world. Everyone must shop for clothes and other necessities. Every culture has sports. All people must learn to adapt to the weather conditions of their environment. Furthermore, civilizations have educational systems so that their youth can continue the beliefs and practices of their ancestors, adapting them to the times. What is different is that these units express a specific author's individual perception of how these cultural phenomena express, embody, and symbolize some of the behavioral and environmental commonalities within the United States. If another person were to write a chapter on the same cultural artifact, it would no doubt be different. Dialogues would be different, readings would be different, even the vocabulary used would be different. This is because, even though culture is shared by a community, each individual's experience with that event is different. For example, not everyone in the United States likes baseball. Others may like it, but only if their favorite team is winning, while others have a passion for the sport that hinges on fanaticism. The point is that these chapters and the views expressed within them should be read with a critical eye, knowing that not everyone in the US shares the exact same viewpoint. To do so would be to stereotype a nation. A book about culture should do the exact opposite: dispel labels and provide a forum for conversation that strives for understanding and that breaks down stereotypes.

Furthermore, this book is not about promoting a US perspective over others. Rather, it is about describing how certain behaviors are enacted in the US. It is meant to provide learners of English some insight into the strange and different ways people of the United States see bathing habits, why they have such strong opinions about guns, and how to navigate a college classroom. The book is meant, if nothing else, to generate discussion and exploration. If *Doing the Transcultural Thing* does this, then the contributors and I have succeeded.

The textbook is not intended to be worked through on a linear basis (i.e., Chapter 1, Chapter 2, Chapter 3, etc.) Vocabulary and structure do not build in sophistication or difficulty from one chapter to the next. The order, though, has been consciously determined to some extent. Having lived and traveled abroad extensively, I know that shopping and eating are two activities that are immediately relevant upon arriving in a new place. Questions about where to get medicine and what's safe or good to eat are constants. Thus, I chose to put these two chapters first. Chapters 3 through 6 are more connected to school and academics. Because this book is for college students studying in an Intensive English Program (IEP), I decided that once the more basic needs of food, clothes, and health have been met, that the school context was the next most relevant. Chapters 7 through 13 concern themselves with other social phenomena that transcend the boundaries of the social and the academic. They contain topics that are relevant to the classroom in many instances while also important to the casual conversation on the bus or around the water cooler. The chapter on baseball, for example, may be more appropriate in spring or early summer during baseball season, while the chapter on winter weather may be best taught in late November or December, just prior to the holiday travel season in the US.

I envision each chapter taking several class periods to work through. Depending on the organization of your language program, it may be that one unit could take as long as a month to get through if your culture class meets once or twice a week. If the class meets more often, then less time will be necessary and if the class meets less frequently, then of course, each unit may require more time to do justice to the content.

Each unit is structured in largely the same way. The chapter begins with student learning outcomes for the unit, warm-up and schemata building questions. Next there are two readings. One reading is an essay about the topic. The other reading may be a poem, model dialogues, or an additional reading with a different focus on the same topic. Before each reading activity, a list of vocabulary is provided. Teachers can decide whether they want to explicitly teach the vocabulary prior to the readings or dialogues or leave this to the students to do on their own. Every attempt has been made to **bold** the first occurrence of each word from the lists in their respective readings. At times, there will be overlap or repetition of the highlighted vocabulary, meaning that multiple chapters may make explicit the same lexical items. I see nothing wrong with this, as the act of learning itself is cyclical.

At the end of each unit, there are suggested activities and various websites for further exploration. It is not necessary to do all of the activities and it is, of course, completely appropriate to create or invoke different activities not listed. Attempts have been made to provide suggestions for different proficiency levels. I am not sure how successful these were as some of the activities listed for "beginning" may be equally appropriate for more advanced proficiency levels.

Originally, I conceived this book to be written at a pseudo-intermediate level so as to be appropriate for multiple levels. This proved to be a challenging and unrealistic goal. Teachers who piloted chapters in their classes have had relative success with them in intermediate levels and up; thus, this is where I would begin.

Finally, a word about the contributors is apropos. First of all, I could not have done this without the contributors. They have all worked hard, exhibited great patience, and produced quality chapters filled with much to discuss. Additionally, each of the contributors has direct and intimate experience with language learning and language teaching. Several of the contributors have extensive experience teaching in IEPs. Some of the contributors were students, themselves, in IEPs prior to earning advanced degrees in the United States. And last but not least, all of the contributors have lived and taught internationally; thus, they are able to empathize with the joys and challenges of doing the transcultural thing.

It is my hope that this work is received favorably and that subsequent editions with additional chapters can be produced. For this reason, I would be delighted to hear from those who have used the text to learn of your experiences, good and bad, and to offer constructive comments that will make future editions that much better and that much more useful.

Enjoy the journey

Michael
mwschwartz@stcloudstate.edu

References

Kramsch, C. (1998). *Language and culture.* Oxford: Oxford University Press.

Scarino, A. (2014). Learning as reciprocal, interpretive meaning-making: A view from collaborative research into the professional learning of teachers of languages. *Modern Language Journal 98*(1), pp. 386–401.

Contributors

Antonio Causarano is currently an Assistant Professor of Education in the Department of Curriculum and Instruction at the University of Mary Washington, VA. He holds a PhD in Education and a MA in Special Education from the University of New Mexico. He also holds a MA in TESOL and Bilingual Education from the University of Findlay, Ohio. Antonio has taught as a special education teacher in New Mexico and taught Italian as a second language at the University of New Mexico, USA.

Pei-ni Causarano, a native of Taiwan, with multilingual and multicultural language backgrounds, has been an enthusiastic language educator for more than fifteen years, serving as an ESL and foreign instructor and consultant at public schools and college levels in the United States and Taiwan. She received her PhD in Educational Linguistics at the University of New Mexico. She loves to travel, study languages, and teach languages. Her research area includes language acquisition, pedagogy, and psycholinguistics, which are inspired by her teaching experience and interactions with students.

Laura Code teaches ESL to new Americans in an adult basic education program. She has a Master's in ESL from Hamline University and received Hamline's Sara Elizabeth Cajamarca award for her master's thesis on culture and pragmatics. She is fluent in Spanish and has traveled throughout Central and South America.

Chris DiStasio has been teaching ESL since 1999. He earned a Master's Degree in Teaching English as a Second Language from the University of Central Missouri in 2005 and has taught ESL in a variety of contexts, from community ESL to university ESL. He currently teaches in the Ohio Program of Intensive English at Ohio University. He specializes in CALL, especially in maintaining a paperless classroom model as well as in computer-based writing, skill development monitoring, classroom management, and error correction techniques. He lived and taught EFL in Istanbul, Turkey, for two years.

Monica Gruber found her love of ESL through Spain's Ministry of Education grant teaching program after graduating from Marquette University. She taught elementary and high school ESL in Madrid for three years before she decided to pursue her TESL Master at St. Cloud State University. Since graduating she teaches English for Specific Purposes at the University of Malaga, Spain. She has always believed in the importance of learning the culture behind the language. This belief has led her to create Online English & Culture Skype classes for aspiring foreign students coming to the US. You can visit her page at mgenglish.com.

Kikuko Omori is currently teaching Intercultural Communication and other Communication courses at St. Cloud State University as a fixed-term faculty member with the rank of Assistant Professor. She is originally from Tokyo, Japan, and fluent in Japanese (her native tongue). She took her ESL courses at the University of Nebraska-Lincoln when she was an exchange student from Senshu University, Japan. Dr. Omori completed her B.A. at Senshu University, Japan in Business Administration. She earned her MA from the University of Kansas in Communication, and her doctoral degree from the University of Wisconsin-Milwaukee in Communication. Much of her research focuses on media and technology influence on human communication processes across cultures. Her work has been published in journals such as *Journal of Intercultural Communication Research, International Journal of Interactive Communication Systems and Technologies,* and *Computers in Human Behavior.*

Michael Schwartz is an Assistant Professor in the MA-TESL program at St. Cloud State University and the Director of the Intensive English Center. He has over twenty five years of experience teaching ESL in intensive English programs both domestically and internationally. Michael teaches graduate classes in World Englishes, Discourse Analysis, and Second Language Writing. His research interests include second language acquisition, identity and language learning, and second language writing. He earned his PhD in Educational Linguistics at the University of New Mexico.

Anna Willson earned an MA in Teaching English as a Second Language at Central Missouri State University (now known as University of Central Missouri). She taught English at a Hungarian school in Cluj-Napoca, Romania, experiencing the beautiful culture of Transylvania for two years. Returning to Missouri, she taught at the English Language Center at CMSU for five years. Since 2004, she has been employed as an instructor with Spring International Language Center at the University of Arkansas, where she has taught all levels of reading, writing, grammar, listening, speaking, TOEFL-prep, and university writing classes.

Moussa Traore, form Burkina Faso in western Africa, has taught both French and English, as well as culture classes, in the Minneapolis/Saint-Paul area where he earned his PhD. He is currently teaching in the Intensive English Center at Saint Cloud State University in Minnesota.

Alexandra Yarbrough has been teaching ESL for four years. She has worked in Ecuador, Colombia, China, South Korea, and is now working with new to country students at a high school in Minnesota. She is currently completing her MA at St. Cloud State University.

Chapter 1

A Penny Saved Is a Penny Earned

Monica Gruber

© John Brueske/Shutterstock.com

Student Learning Objectives

By the end of this unit, students will be able to:

- ► Understand the different kinds of stores in the US.
- ► Make informed decisions about the best type of store for their particular food or clothing needs.
- ► Identify over-the-counter medicines and the best places to purchase them.
- ► Understand the concept and use of coupons.

Warm-Up Questions

1. In your country are there certain days of the week when the stores are closed?
2. In your country where do you buy your over-the-counter medicines? Are they always the same price no matter where you buy them? Where do you think you would buy them here in the United States? Make a list of local stores that might sell over-the-counter medicines.
3. What are coupons? Have you used coupons before? Do you think saving and using coupons can really save you money?
4. Can you negotiate the price of food or clothing products in your country? Is negotiating an expected behavior? Are there places where you cannot negotiate? Can you negotiate prices in the US?
5. Have you heard of sales tax? Do you have sales tax on products in your country? How much is the sales tax in the state you're in now? Does sales tax apply to all items purchased in your state? Is sales tax included in the marked prices at the store?
6. What do you think the title of this chapter means? Do you have a similar expression in your language?

Take a few minutes to think about the questions above. Write down your answers and then find a partner and share your answers. Do you and your partner come from countries where shopping practices differ? Now, let's find more out about shopping in the States.

READING 1

Vocabulary

Grocery store (np)	Toiletries (n)	Convenience (n)
Produce (n)	Crossbreed (n)	Expiration date (np)
Over-the-counter (adj)	Affordable (adj)	Lower-end (adj)
Take advantage of (vp)	Prescription (n)	Budget (n)
Groceries (n)	Coupon (n)	Convenience store (np)
Generic brand (np)	Department store (np)	In the long run (pp)
Require (v)	Add up (vp)	

© LuckyPhoto/Shutterstock.com

© Lisa S./Shutterstock.com

Complex Solutions to Simple Problems

1   You are finally settled in your new apartment when your stomach starts to grumble. The next
2   question is where to go for food, which depends on what kind of food you're looking for and how
3   much you plan on spending. Just like popular clothing brands, **grocery stores** come in all shapes and
4   sizes and depending on your wallet you'll want to choose wisely. Your local supermarket will offer you
5   the widest range of food products. It's best to ask a fellow classmate or teacher where they shop to get
6   an idea of what your city has to offer. Hypermarkets are the **crossbreed** between a supermarket and a
7   **department store**. They are usually gigantic and can offer everything from clothes, electronics,
8   **groceries**, to bicycles. A couple of examples of hypermarkets in the US are Wal-Mart and Target.
9   Remember you get what you pay for, so a **lower-end** store like Wal-Mart may be cheaper but the
10 quality may suffer. You may find groceries, especially **produce**, in the States to be much more
11 expensive than in your home country. It's important to understand that grocery stores usually carry a
12 **generic brand** of most products that offers a more **affordable** option. For example you can buy
13 Nabisco Oreo's for $2.98 or buy Wal-Mart's Great Value Chocolate Twist & Shout Sandwich Cookies for
14 $1.98. That's a $1 difference, which may seem small but it **adds up** fast! Plan your **budget** before you
15 leave your house and make sure you don't forget your pre-planned grocery list.

© sumroeng chinnapan/Shutterstock.com

16   Many **over-the-counter** medicines can be found in grocery stores and discount stores. Over-the-
17 counter medicines are the common meds that do not **require** a doctor's **prescription**. The most
18 common are painkillers, anti-acids, cold and flu medicines, and other medicines for common ailments.
19 These medicines can be found at different prices depending on where they are purchased. For example:
20 buying cough medicine at the university bookstore or **convenience store** may be twice the price
21 compared to buying it at your local pharmacy, Wal-Mart, or supermarket. In the States you pay for
22 **convenience**. However, when you are feeling sick and you are desperate to feel better, paying a little
23 more may be worth it. The best advice is to prepare by buying the basic over-the-counter meds ahead
24 of time. Talk with the onsite pharmacist and ask them to show you the different options for the
25 common cold and other illnesses. By doing this you can even **take advantage of** the coupons stores
26 send to your mailbox or offer directly at the store.

© EasterBunny/Shutterstock.com

27 Just like medicine, common **toiletries** also vary in price according to where they are sold. Toilet
28 paper, tissue, toothpaste, shaving cream, shampoo, soap, laundry detergent, etc., can probably be
29 purchased at the local university bookstore, but these items will be much more expensive there than at
30 a discount store or local grocery store. For example, Tide, a popular laundry detergent, might cost
31 $10.00 for 32 ounces at the university bookstore or convenience store, but at Wal-Mart, the same size
32 container of Tide might only cost $6.00, a $4.00 savings. So, unless there is no choice, it's best to shop
33 for toiletries and other necessities at a discount store. Another way to save money is to clip **coupons**.
34 Coupons are sales the stores offer. Coupons can be found in newspapers, on the Internet, and
35 sometimes a store will send coupons through the mail. It's possible to find coupons for common
36 medicines, toiletries, food, and even for restaurants. For example, if you need to buy toothpaste, you
37 can probably find a coupon for Crest or Colgate brand toothpaste. The coupon may be for 50 cents off
38 or more. Be careful though, it's important to read the coupon very closely because the store will only
39 accept a coupon for the exact item listed on the coupon. Also, coupons have **expiration dates**. Be sure
40 the coupon you are using has not expired because the store will not accept it if it is too old. If you
41 present the little piece of paper with the offer on it when checking out, the cashier will then reduce the
42 amount of the item by the amount listed on the coupon. Coupons can save you a lot of money **in the**
43 **long run**, but cutting them out and organizing them is a time-consuming process. It's a great way to
44 practice your reading and learn new vocabulary while saving yourself money!

© Carolyn Franks/Shutterstock.com

© Vanatchanan/Shutterstock.com

Comprehension/Discussion Questions

1. What simple problems are mentioned in the reading?
2. What does the term "Generic brand" mean in line 14? What are the benefits & disadvantages of buying such products?
3. What does the author encourage you to do before you get sick?
4. What is the purpose of coupons? Do you have coupons in your country? What things can you use coupons for?
5. What are toiletries? Where is the best place to purchase them?

Comprehension/Vocabulary Questions

1. What is the main idea of this reading?
   a) Where to find a deal on toiletries.
   b) How Americans grocery shop.
   c) The different store options and prices of common goods.
   d) How to save money shopping for your common goods in the States.

2. Which of the following is a synonym for "grocery store" in line 3?
   a) Department stores
   b) Supermarkets
   c) Gas stations
   d) Shopping centers

3. List the different kinds of stores mentioned in the reading.
   a)
   b)
   c)
   d)
   e)
   f)

4. Which of the following can be synonyms for "produce" as it is used in line 10?
   a) make
   b) meat
   c) fruits & vegetables
   d) do

5. What does "affordable" mean on line 12?
   a) A cheaper option
   b) A more expansive option
   c) A more expensive option
   d) A smarter option

6. List the different kinds of over-the-counter medicines and discuss the appropriate situations when to take each one.

7. What does "require" mean in line 17?

a) Dislike
b) Need
c) Want
d) Have

8. Do coupons have expiration dates?
a) Yes
b) No
c) Sometimes

9. Where can you find coupons?
a) Internet
b) Your mailbox
c) Newspapers
d) In-store
e) All of the above

10. Do you pay for convenience in your country like here in the States? Explain.

READING 2

Vocabulary

Closet (n)	Percentage (n)	Racks (n)
Secondhand (adj)	Sift (v)	Outlet malls
Merchandise (n)	Deals (n, v)	At this point (pp)
Cheaper (adj)	Cost me a fortune (vp)	Handpick (v)
Treasure hunt (n)	Slightly (adv)	Reused (n, v)
Freezing (adj)	Bed sheets (np)	Sweater (n)
Consignment store (np)		

© Christina Richards/Shutterstock.com

© June Marie Sobrito/Shutterstock.com

Dialogue: One Man's Trash Is Another Man's Treasure

Moving thousands of miles away from home most likely includes adjusting to changes in weather and even seasons. These differences in weather call for changes in your **closet** in order to be prepared for the new temperatures. Let's see how Amy and Samir figure out the best way to dress for cold, snowy winters.

1	Samir:	I'm **freezing**. I didn't realize how cold it would be. I need all new clothes.
2	Amy:	Yeah, it took me a couple months to buy all the new winter clothes I needed before I was
3		comfortable again. It **cost me a fortune** buying everything new.
4	Samir:	**At this point** I don't care what I spend. I just want to feel warm again. I feel like I'm literally
5		freezing the minute I walk outside. Where can I go to buy everything I need?
6	Amy:	After talking with my teacher I realized that **secondhand** and **consignment stores** are really
7		popular. You can buy **slightly** used clothes for so much less than at the regular stores.
8	Samir:	Really? What's the difference between the two kinds of stores?
9	Amy:	Consignment stores usually have nicer, more current, and higher quality items. The
10		consignment store **handpicks** the **merchandise** they are willing to sell. The people who donate
11		their clothes to the store then receive a **percentage** of the purchase. This is why their prices are
12		usually higher than secondhand stores.
13	Samir:	Used clothes? I don't know…
14	Amy:	Have you ever stayed at a hotel before?
15	Samir:	Yes, of course.
16	Amy:	Well, the **bed sheets** weren't new. They've been used by MANY people and then washed and
17		**reused**. It's the same idea. When I need another sweater, I buy it secondhand.
18	Sami:	That's interesting. Can I get shoes secondhand too?
19	Amy:	I'm not sure I'd buy used shoes. That might really damage your feet.
20	Samir:	Ok, so secondhand stores are **cheaper** but what about the style of the clothes?
21	Amy:	Well, there's a little of everything. You have to **sift** through the **racks** of tops and **sweaters** but
22		it's worth it!
23	Samir:	Ok, maybe I'll give it a chance. The next time you go let me know.
24	Amy:	Sure, no problem. It's definitely an experience the first time you go but think of it as a **treasure**
25		**hunt**. You have to dig but sometimes there are real **deals** on top designers and brands. You
26		never know what you're gonna find.
27	Samir:	I've got to buy so many things that it's probably a good idea to save where I can. Do you know
28		where I can find a secondhand store?
29	Amy:	There's a Salvation Army Store just across from the movie theater in town. You can take the
30		bus. It goes right by the store.
31	Samir:	Oh, that's nice.
32	Amy:	You can also find deals on new clothes at outlet malls if the idea of wearing used clothing
33		doesn't convince you.
34	Samir:	What's the difference between outlet malls and regular shopping malls?
35	Amy:	Top brands like Nike or Gap send last season's styles to their outlet stores and sell them at a
36		discounted price. A lot of times they sell last season's winter clothes at the beginning of
37		summer for really cheap! You can plan ahead and buy great coats, sweaters, & boots for next
38		winter.
39	Samir:	Where can I find an outlet store?
40	Amy:	They usually group them together and create outlet malls. So, it's really easy to get in a day of
41		outlet shopping at all your favorite stores. Let's Google it and find our nearest outlet mall. Do
42		you want to go this weekend?
43	Samir:	Yes! I'll drive!

Discussion Questions

1. Do secondhand stores exist in your home countries? Are they popular? What do you think about the concept of them?
2. Did you have to buy new clothes when you moved to your new school? About how much did you spend on your new items?
3. Describe the differences between secondhand stores and consignment stores?.
4. Would you consider purchasing secondhand (used) clothing? Why or why not? What items would you prefer to buy new? Share your list with a partner.
5. What is Amy's comparison in lines 20–24? Do you agree with her? Why or why not?
6. What are some inconveniences of shopping at secondhand stores?
7. Do you think Samir will give secondhand shopping a try? What makes you think that?
8. Where would you prefer to shop?

Comprehension/Vocabulary Questions

1. What is Samir's principle problem?
   a) He wants to help Amy shop.
   b) He is very hot.
   c) He's not prepared for the weather.
   d) He wants to buy name brand clothing.

2. What does the phrase "cost me a fortune" mean in line 3?
   a) Cost a little
   b) Cost an arm and a leg
   c) Cost a normal amount
   d) Cost a little more than usual

3. List the different places to buy clothing mentioned in the reading.
   a)
   b)
   c)
   d)

4. Where do you usually find better quality and brands of clothing?
   a) Secondhand stores
   b) Consignment stores

5. What is a synonym of "sift" in line 21?
   a) Search
   b) Run around
   c) Try on
   d) Find out

6. What does treasure hunt mean as it is used in lines 24–25?

Activities

All levels

▶ Plan a class potluck. Teach your classmates about your favorite dish from your home country. Research where you can possibly find the necessary ingredients: ethnic food stores, gourmet grocery stores, local farmers' markets, regular grocery stores. What coupons can you find for the food items you want to buy?

▶ With your classmates, make a list of the different kinds of clothes people wear for the different seasons (spring, summer, autumn, and winter). Then, brainstorm with your teacher where you can buy these clothes in your community.

▶ Divide the class into groups (3 to 4 in each group). Tell each group they have $150 to buy clothes for the upcoming season. Ask each group to make a list of the clothes they need to buy, where they are going to buy the clothes and how much each clothing item costs. Caveat: Have the groups make a list of clothes they are going to buy and then provide the cost of each item from a department store, a consignment shop, and a thrift store.

Beginning

▶ Make a list of the ingredients needed to make a dish from your home country. Now explain the recipe step-by-step to the class. Brainstorm cooking vocabulary as a class beforehand.

▶ Where are you buying your groceries now? Compare your answers with the class. Explain what you like about the store and what you do not like. As a class figure out the best places to buy groceries and over-the-counter medicines in your area.

▶ Bring in coupons from the stores you shop at (from your mailbox, directly from the store, or from the Internet). What items did you find coupons for? What items could you not find coupons for? What are your coupons offering, for what store(s), what is the expiration date? Be prepared to describe your coupons to your classmates. Caveat: The teacher can bring in several coupons and ask students to identify the exact item, the amount of savings, who will accept the coupon, and the expiration date for each coupon.

Intermediate

▶ How would you describe yourself as a shopper? Are you a bargain hunter? Describe your shopping habits to the class.

▶ Research and locate the Secondhand/Thrift Stores & Consignment stores in your area. Make plans to visit at least one and report back to your class your observations: what you liked, what you didn't like, what you bought, the deals you saw, who was shopping there, etc. Would you recommend this store to your classmates and friends?

Advanced

▶ Research & share the differences between consignment stores and secondhand/thrift stores. Find your local options.

▶ Make 3 debate teams: Team 1 Consignment Stores, Team 2 Secondhand Stores & Team 3 Regular (full price) Stores. Team 1 & 2 will present their 3 reasons why their stores are better. Each team then offers a rebuttal to the opposing team's reasons. The class votes on the winner of the debate. Then the winner and Team 3 debate.

► Listen to the following segment from NPR "Person-To-Person Sales Outlets Succeeding" http://www.npr.org/templates/story/story.php?storyId=101944903
Take notes on the segment and be prepared to talk about it in class. What websites were mentioned in the recording? Divide the class into groups focusing on one website per group. Groups will become "experts" on their pages and present their findings to the class.

Chapter 2

To Eat and Run: What Is American Food?

Chris DiStasio

© alphaspirit/Shutterstock.com

Student Learning Objectives

By the end of this unit, students will be able to:

- ▶ Talk about food from their countries.
- ▶ Talk about the varieties of food found in the US.
- ▶ Understand food options found in the US.
- ▶ Describe different places people can buy food in the US.
- ▶ Read and understand nutrition labels in English.
- ▶ Make informed decisions about their food choices.

Warm-Up Questions

Take a few minutes to think about the questions below. Write down your answers and then find a partner and share your answers.

1. What do you usually eat for breakfast, lunch, and dinner in your country?
2. What are the most popular foods in your country?
3. Where do people shop for food in your country?
4. What do you think American food is?
5. What is fast-food and does your country have fast-food?
6. Where can you find healthy food in your country?
7. When you want to eat food from your country, where can you go?
8. What kinds of food originated in the United States?
9. What do you think the title means? Do people do this in your country?

READING 1

Vocabulary

Raw (adj)	Whole food (np)	Organic (adj)
Greasy (adj)	Protein (n)	Toxic (adj)
Fatty (adj)	Dairy (n)	Fertilizer (n)
Fresh (adj)	Grains (n)	Pesticide (n)
Variety (n)	Calorie (n)	Conventional (adj)
Define (v)	Cholesterol (n)	Farmer's Market (np)
Processed (adj)	Trans fat (n)	Collection (n)
Scratch (n)	Portion (n)	Originated (n)
Grocery shopping (np)	Supermarket (n)	Featuring (adj)
Multiple (adj)	Grocery store (n)	Cuisine (n)
Ingredient (n)	Produce (n)	Dish (n)

© El Nariz/Shutterstock.com

© Smit/Shutterstock.com

© Olga Nayashkova/Shutterstock.com

Dialogue 1

1	Jin:	I'm so tired of American food!
2	Ahmed:	What do you mean?
3	Jin:	I mean it seems like the only thing the cafeteria has is fried chicken, hamburgers, pizza, and
4		peanut butter and jelly. And the only vegetables I can get are cold or **raw**. We eat cooked
5		vegetables in China, not raw.
6	Ahmed:	But American food is many things, not just **greasy fatty** food.
7	Jin:	Like what?
8	Pedro:	Well, there's Chinese food, Mexican food, Indian food ...
9	Jin:	But those are not American ... those are from other countries. I'm Chinese and the Chinese
10		food here is not the same as it is back home.
11	Pedro:	Of course it isn't. I'm from Mexico and I feel the same way, but that's the beauty of American
12		food. It comes from everywhere and you can eat different things every day.
13	Jin:	Man, I'm confused!

Related Discussion Questions

1. Why is Jin confused?
2. What does Jin assume about American food?
3. Do you agree with Pedro that Chinese, Mexican, and Indian food are American food? Why, why not?

© Lesya Dolyuk/Shutterstock.com   © wong yu liang/Shutterstock.com   © bonchan/Shutterstock.com

Dialogue 2

14	Ipek:	I miss food from my country!
15	Bedoor:	I know what you mean. When I first came here, I gained a lot of weight because I couldn't
16		find anything that I was used to. American food is so greasy with all the pizza, hamburgers,
17		French fries, and fried chicken. It's all so fatty. I really missed cuscus and chicken.
18	Ipek:	What did you do?
19	Bedoor:	I asked some of my Saudi friends, and they told me about a market in the city that sells halal
20		food. It really saved me. I know I've seen Turkish food in there too. I'll email the address.
21	Ipek:	Thanks!
22	Bedoor:	We should also talk about what kinds of American foods you might like.
23	Ipek:	That would be great, but I don't know if I'll ever like American food. It is so greasy and full of
24		chemicals. And it's just not **fresh**. I love fresh food.

25 Bedoor: But there's a lot of **variety** in American food, and not all of it is unhealthy. If you'd like I can
26 help you find better American food.
27 Ipek: That would be really nice. Can we go to the store together?
28 Bedoor: Of course! We can go **grocery** shopping tomorrow.

Related Discussion Questions

1. What problem does Ipek have?
2. How does Bedoor help Ipek with her problem?

© BlueSkyImage/Shutterstock.com

© Subbotina Anna/Shutterstock.com

READING 2

What Is American Food

1 People who come to the United States for the first time think that fast-food **defines** American food. How-
2 ever, fast-food is only part of American food culture.
3 Although fast-food restaurants are common, fast-food does not make up most of what Americans
4 usually eat. Many Americans cook food at home. Sometimes that means just heating up **processed** food
5 in a microwave, but some people still cook from **scratch**, using **multiple ingredients** and **whole foods**.
6 Some Americans follow the idea of the *five basic food groups*: **protein** such as meat, legumes, and nuts;
7 **dairy** (ex., milk, eggs, and cheese); **grains** (ex., rice and wheat); **fruits;** and **vegetables.** Health profes-
8 sionals and the government recommend that everyone eat food from each food group every day.

(Source: http://www.choosemyplate.gov/downloads/mini_poster_English_final.pdf)

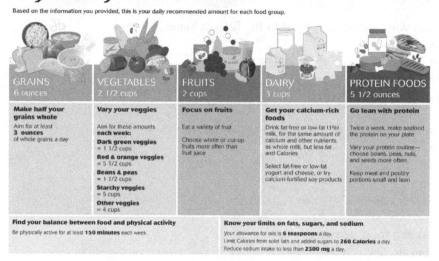

(Source: http://www.choosemyplate.gov/supertracker-tools/daily-food-plans.html)

9   While the food in fast-food restaurants is often high in **calories, cholesterol,** and **trans fats,** fast-
10   food restaurants are starting to offer healthier choices. For example, at McDonald's, Wendy's, Burger
11   King, Subway, and Starbucks, you can get salads, fruit and yogurt, or oatmeal. Most sit-down restaurants,
12   like Applebee's or Denny's, offer healthy meal options too. These are sometimes found in a special section
13   of the menu, labeled as *light,* or there may be a picture of a heart next to a menu item. American restau-
14   rants also like to serve large **portions** of food. If Americans leave a restaurant still feeling hungry, they
15   don't think they got what they paid for and may not recommend the restaurant to others.

16   Healthy food options are available at **supermarkets** or **grocery stores.** You just have to look for them.
17   Grocery stores have lots of fresh **produce** (fruits and vegetables), grains, and meats year-round. Further-
18   more, it is common to find special aisles for **organic** foods, or food that is grown without the use of **toxic**
19   chemicals such as **fertilizers** and **pesticides**. Many people feel that organic food is healthier because it is
20   more natural.

21   Although **conventional** grocery stores now sell healthier choices, there are specialty grocery stores
22   that sell mostly organic food. Examples of these stores are Whole Foods, Sprouts, and Trader Joe's.

23   In addition to supermarkets and grocery stores, **farmer's markets** offer a variety of healthy food
24   choices. A farmer's market is an area of a town or city where locally grown and produced fruits, vegeta-
25   bles, meat, grains, and homemade items such as jams, breads, soaps, and more are sold. Many farmer's
26   markets are only open on Saturday, and most only operate during late spring, summer, and early fall.

27   So "What is American food?" It might best be described as a **collection** of different kinds of food
28   that **originated** from other parts of the world, but that has been adapted. As American culture is made
29   up of a wide variety of individual, original cultures, American food is made up of a wide variety of dishes
30   that come from those cultures. For example, restaurants **featuring** Mexican, Italian, and Chinese **cuisine**
31   are very common in the US, even in small towns. It is important to understand that although these kinds
32   of cuisines are called Mexican, Italian, Chinese, etc., the flavors, ingredients, and kinds of dishes may be
33   quite different from what is found in Mexico, Italy, or China.

34   All in all, while there are a lot of fast-food restaurants in the US, and Americans eat a lot of fast-food,
35   it is incorrect to think of American food as being only something that comes from McDonald's or Pizza
36   Hut. Just as the English language has borrowed words from many different languages and cultures,
37   American food has borrowed from the great and wonderful flavors of the world, adapted them, and cre-
38   ated unique **dishes** which can only be described as one thing: American food.

Reading Comprehension

1. Where can you find healthy food in the United States?
   a) Grocery stores
   b) Fast-food restaurants
   c) Farmer's markets
   d) All of the above

2. What kinds of healthy food items can be found in fast-food restaurants?
   a) Hamburgers
   b) Pizza
   c) Salads
   d) Fried chicken

3. What makes a food item organic?
   a) Chemicals
   b) Artificial ingredients
   c) Fertilizers
   d) Grown naturally

4. Mexican and Chinese food in the United States is the same as it is in Mexico and China.
   a) True
   b) False

5. List the five basic food groups.
   a) _____
   b) _____
   c) _____
   d) _____
   e) _____

6. Which of the following can you find in a farmer's market?
   a) Fresh vegetables
   b) Fresh fruit
   c) Homemade bread
   d) All of the above

Vocabulary Questions

1. What is a synonym for **define** as it is used in line 1?
   a) Describe
   b) Tell
   c) Call
   d) See

2. If a person cooks a meal from **scratch** (line 5), what do they do?
   a) Heat it in a microwave
   b) Buy it at a fast food restaurant
   c) Make it at home with fresh ingredients
   d) Make it at home with lots of grease and fat

3. What are you likely to find in the **produce** (line 17) aisle of a grocery store?
   a) Fruits and vegetables
   b) Eggs and cheese
   c) Meat and legumes
   d) Dairy products

4. What can you buy in a **farmer's market** (line 23)?
   a)
   b)
   c)
   d)

5. What is a synonym for **cuisine** as it is used in line 30?
   a) Ethnic food
   b) American food
   c) Food
   d) Dinner

6. What word below is <u>NOT</u> a synonym of **feature** as it is used in line 30?
   a) Serve
   b) Offer
   c) Have
   d) Collect

7. A dish with a **variety** of ingredients has **multiple** ingredients.
   a) True
   b) False

8. **Dish** as it is used in line 38 means_____.
   a) Plate
   b) Special
   c) Meal
   d) Culture

Suggested Activities

All Levels

▶ Ask your teacher or look around at local newspapers and events bulletin boards to find a local church or other religious organization that is sponsoring a dinner. Churches and other religious organizations in the United States often have community outreach events such as dinners. It can be a very good opportunity to try American food that is not fast-food and to talk to native speakers. Then make the experience into a presentation to give the class or a writing assignment. Consider these questions:

Where are you from?
Where do you live?
What are your favorite kinds of food?
What is American food?

▶ Eat at an American sit-down restaurant for dinner where you are served by a waiter/waitress. Notice what is different and similar about the points below.

Was your food server a man or a woman?
How was the service different from the service in your home country?
What food items on the menu are familiar to you?
What food items on the menu are not familiar to you?
Did you leave a tip for the food server?

▶ Check this website that shows how many fast-food restaurants are located in the fifty states in the United States: https://www.yahoo.com/food/every-state-in-the-usa-ranked-by-its-fast-food-10990072 2996.html. Have students compare the state they are living in with other states. Are there fast-food restaurants that are not in the state they are living in that they would like to have? Then discuss with the whole class, small group members, or a partner how the state you live in compares with other states. Are you surprised by how your state is ranked? Are you surprised by other states you may know about?

▶ Perform a web search for "original American food" and then discuss what you found. Have you had any of these foods? Are you surprised to find out that the foods are originally American? Sometimes there is controversy about whether some foods are originally American or not, so regarding those who say these foods are not really American originals, where do the foods supposedly come from? The results of the web search can be made into a presentation to give the class or into a writing assignment.

▶ Have students perform a web search for a popular American restaurant and find the restaurant's "nutrition chart" (for example, you could do a search for "McDonald's nutrition chart") and then discuss what you find. Which food items seem to be the healthiest? Why? Which food items seem to be the least healthy? Why?

▶ Have students brainstorm a fast-food restaurant that would serve foods from their country. What would the foods be? How would the food be served so that people can eat it on the run? Have students give a presentation, make a video or PowerPoint of their fast-food restaurant. The presentation should include not only food but the nutritional information also.

Beginning

▶ Go to a local supermarket or grocery store and purchase a kind of food—a natural or processed food—that you have never had before. Ask people who work at the supermarket or grocery store and/ or a friend about how the food is used by Americans. Then make the experience into a presentation to give to the class, and consider sharing it among your class members. Consider these questions for the presentation:

How does the food taste?
What does the food smell like?
How is the food typically used by Americans?
If the food is processed, what are the ingredients in the food?

Intermediate/Advanced

Reading a Nutritional Label

Packaged food has at least two labels on them: (1) **ingredients labels,** and (2) **nutritional labels.** The ingredients section tells people exactly what is in the package and what if anything has been added to the food. For example, on a can of tomato soup, the ingredients might be tomatoes, water, high fructose corn syrup, flour, corn starch, salt, and natural flavorings. The ingredients label tells people how **natural** or **artificial** the food they are buying really is. This label can also be very important to people who have special diets or who have food allergies.

There's also a nutritional label on all packaged foods. The nutritional label shows how much of certain nutrients are found in a food item. Some nutrients, such as **fat**, **vitamins** and **minerals**, **fiber**, and protein, are generally considered healthy and desirable. Some nutrients, such as **saturated fat**, cholesterol, **sodium**, and **sugars**, are generally considered unhealthy, so trying to limit these is a good idea. Here is an example of a nutritional label:

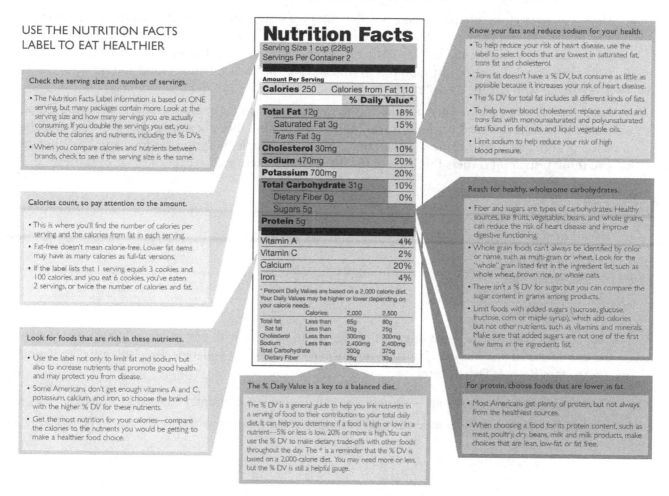

(Source: http://www.choosemyplate.gov/downloads/NutritionFactsLabel.pdf)

Discuss with the class about the different information found on the nutritional label. Do packaged foods in your country have similar labels? How are they the same? How are they different?

Have students check out the food labels at home or in a grocery store. Students can research the label on the container or the item for nutrients and the amounts as well as which ingredients are natural and which are artificial. Have them compare a product that is labeled "organic" with the same product that isn't organic. Have students give a presentation on their findings.

▶   Go to a local farmer's market. Take notes about what you see and hear. Make sure to speak to as many native English speakers as possible. Although farmer's markets are good places to ask a stranger survey questions, you may feel nervous in doing so. If you feel too nervous to talk to just anyone there, keep in mind that vendors at a farmer's market usually want to talk to you because they are happy to talk to customers about their products. Then make the experience into a presentation to give the class or a writing assignment. Consider these questions:

How long have you been in business?
Where is your farm/business?
What do you grow/produce?
Is your produce/are your products organic?
Can you tell me about the benefits of organic farming?

▶ Have a grocery store role-play. Some possible roles are store clerk, customer, cashier, store manager, and security guard. Students who have the role of customer could make a grocery list from a picture dictionary, especially items that are not very familiar, and then ask the student who has the role of store clerk about the items (for example, in which department each item is found and how it is used). The student who has the role of manager could be asked if the store clerk cannot help.

▶ Food trucks have become very popular in the United States recently. Have students investigate food trucks in their area. Are there food trucks? Why do you think they are so popular? How are they the same or different from fast-food restaurants? Where are people likely to find food trucks? What do you think restaurant owners think about food trucks? Are there food trucks in other countries?

Advanced

▶ Have students watch one of the food documentaries listed below.

○ Food Inc.
○ Supersize Me
○ Forks over Knives
○ Food Matters

Then have a class debate about organic farming versus farming with pesticides and fertilizers. Here is an excellent, comprehensive Internet resource about making a debate in class http://iteslj.org/ Techniques/Krieger-Debate.html.

▶ Give a presentation or write an essay comparing food from your country to food in America.

▶ Give a presentation or write an essay about eating at restaurants in your country and in America.

Chapter 3

Learn the Ropes: U.S. Classroom Culture

Antonio Causarano and Pei-Ni Lin Causarano

© villorejo/Shutterstock.com

Student Learning Objectives

By the end of this unit, students will be able to:

- ▶ Describe some of the differences between classroom culture in their country and the US.
- ▶ Understand how US classroom culture influences curriculum and instruction.
- ▶ Understand US classroom expectations, interactional practices, and grading systems in the US.
- ▶ Use strategies for clear and specific communication with faculty and staff.

Warm-Up Questions

1. What is the usual way of teaching in your country? Do you listen to professors or do students work in groups?
2. How do students ask questions in class in your country?
3. What are common ways for students to meet professors in your country?
4. How are you graded in your countries? Do you take tests, write papers, or work with other students?
5. Do students ever give presentations in class in your country?
6. What do you think the title: *Learn the Ropes* means?

Take a few minutes to think about the questions above. Write down your answers and then find a partner to share your answers. Do you and your partner come from countries with similar institutions of higher education? If not, what are the differences you find in studying in higher education in your countries?

READING 1

Vocabulary

Centralization (adj)	Influential (adj)	Fate (n)
Independent (adj)	Juxtapose (v)	Mirror (v)
Curriculum (n)	Colonist (n)	Collapse (n)
Govern (v)	Missionary (n)	Conflict (v)
Standard (n)	Listen in (vp)	Relevant (adj)
Hire (v)	Ultimately (adv)	Learner-centered (adj)
Lecture (n)	Disgrace (v)	
Group (np)	Prevent (v)	

© Konstantin L/Shutterstock.com

© Jorge Salcedo/Shutterstock.com

© Arturo Limon/Shutterstock.com

Overview of the US System of Higher Education

US Education System

- There are many different kinds of schools in the US. There are community colleges, technical colleges, state universities, and research universities. Some schools are private and some are public. Their **curriculums** are similar but different.

- These different schools are **independent** of each other but each helps to support the other.

- The US Department of Education can influence schools, but does not **govern** them.

- Students have some flexibility in their plan of study. Students can change degree programs even after they have begun their study plan.

- Admission **standards** are different for each school. Each school decides what a student needs to know and be able to do for admission.

- Faculty members are hired by individual schools. A school decides what they need and then advertises for faculty to apply. It is a competitive process.

Non-US Education System

- In many countries, there is one department in the government that controls all the schools. This is called **centralization**. All schools use the same curriculum.

- The administration of schools is governed by a national ministry of education.

- Students choose a fixed plan of study and usually cannot make changes in their plan of study once they have begun.

- Standardized/national admission tests are given each year, usually in the spring or early summer. A student's performance on these tests can determine where the student goes to college.

- Faculty members are **hired by** individual schools. Faculty must be certified and demonstrate credentials and quality of references.

The above comparison between US colleges and universities and other countries is very general. Discuss the questions below with a partner:

1. How is higher education governed in your country?
2. What are the advantages and disadvantages of both systems?

© Monkey Business Images/Shutterstock.com

The usual way of teaching and learning in many countries is **lecture.** Students listen to the professor, take notes, and prepare for a test later in the semester or at the end of the year. There is usually no interaction with the professor or any group work. What is the usual teaching and learning style in your country? Here is a typical classroom scenario found in many countries:

Scenario 1: Introduction to Literature

Professor: Good Morning. How are you doing today?

Students: *(students all stand and say)* "Very well. Thank you."

Professor: I will talk about the importance of Literature in our modern times.

Students: *(Listening, usually in a large class of 100 or more students or auditorium, and begin taking notes.)*

Professor: *(Begins lecturing):* Today I'm going to talk about Chinua Achebe, who wrote *Things Fall Apart,* the famous and highly **influential** book about Nigeria. In Achebe's book, he tells the story of Okonkwo, a man from an Ibo village. He **juxtaposes** Okonkwo's fall from one of respect and community influence to disgrace with the arrival of European **colonists** and the ultimate destruction of the Ibo culture by European **Missionaries.**

© Monkey Business Images/Shutterstock.com

11   The expectation in these educational systems is not to question or criticize but to memorize the facts and
12   concepts the professor lectures about. This kind of classroom is often called **teacher-centered** and is what
13   is known as top-down because the teacher tells students what they need to know that the teacher believes
14   is important. Students do not question, critique, or discover on their own or in a small group.
15   The following is an example of how some professors in the US might approach the same literature
16   class.

Scenario 2: US Course Introduction to English Literature

17   Professor: Good Morning. How is everyone?

18   Students: *(sitting)* Fine. Thanks.

19   Professor: Okay, today we're gonna get into **groups** of 4 or 5. In your groups, you need to discuss the
20   questions prepared for Chinhua Achebe's *Things Fall Apart.* One member of your group needs
21   to take notes of your discussion. One member needs to summarize the chapters that were
22   assigned for today. You will have 25 minutes to discuss the questions. Then at the end of the
23   discussion time, each group will present on one question. Decide on who will talk for your
24   group. We will then end with a whole class conversation about Okonkwo and the arrival of the
25   European missionaries. Here are the questions. I'll come around and **listen in** while you're in
26   your groups.

27   Students: *(form groups, while the professor hands out the questions).*

Questions

1. Describe how Okonkwo **ultimately** ended up being **disgraced** in his Ibo village.
2. What happened and what if anything could Okonkwo have done to **prevent** his **fate**?
3. How does Okonkwo's fate **mirror** that of the **collapse** of Nigerian culture when the European Missionaries arrive?
4. What promises do the missionaries bring and how do these "promises" **conflict** with the cultures of Nigeria?
5. Was there anything that Okonkwo and the other villages could have done to prevent the ultimate collapse of village culture in Nigeria?
6. How is *Things Fall Apart* **relevant** to our lives today in the twenty-first century?

28   Professor: *(25 minutes later) Okay, Group 1, can you tell the class what you came up with for question A?*

29   Students in Group 1: Well we, think that Okonkwo was a victim of the times. He . . .

Discussion Questions

1. How are the two classes different? How are they the same?
2. Which format (lecture or group work) is most familiar to you? Which one do you think is better? Why?
3. What are the benefits to the lecture format and what are the benefits of the group work format? What are the negative effects about each class format?

READING 2

Vocabulary

Philosophy (n)
Liberal (adj)
Exposure (n)
Perspective (n)
Well-rounded (adj)

Surround (n)
Bachelor's degree (n)
Associate's Degree (n)
Doctoral Degree (n)
Confer (v)

Practical experience (n)
Internship (n)
Mission (n)

Differences among Institutions of Higher Education in the US

1 Institutions of higher education in the US have different **missions** and **philosophies** of education. The
2 offering of courses, specializations, and course of study can oftentimes leave international students con-
3 fused and uncertain about what courses to take and what to study. In very general terms, there are three
4 types of higher education institutions in the US: community college, liberal arts college, and university.

Community College

© Cynthia Farmer/Shutterstock.com

5   Community colleges are also sometimes called *Junior Colleges, Technical Colleges,* or *two-year colleges.*
6   Community colleges focus on training people to do specific jobs, such as nursing, dental hygiene, auto
7   mechanic, secretarial work, appliance repair, computer programming, electrician, and more. The mis-
8   sion of a community college is to prepare people for the workforce in areas that the local community
9   needs. If a student graduates from a community college, the student will earn an Associate's Degree.
10 Degrees usually take about 2 years to complete.

Liberal Arts College

© Stephen B. Goodwin/Shutterstock.com

11   A **liberal** arts college tries to give students a general education in many different subjects, including
12   anthropology, art, business, biology, chemistry, education, history, foreign language, literature, music,
13   psychology, sociology, theater, and more. A liberal arts college will usually require students to have about
14   60 credit hours, or half of their undergraduate education, across multiple areas. The belief is that **expo-**
15   **sure** to many different subjects and **perspectives** will make for a more **well-rounded** person who has
16   some knowledge and experience with many things that **surround** our lives. Students who graduate from
17   a liberal arts college will earn a Bachelor's Degree. Most liberal arts colleges only offer a 4-year Bachelor's
18   Degree.

University

© holbox/Shutterstock.com

19   A university has a dual mission: education and research. A university offers degrees in many different
20   subjects. A university will often times overlap with a liberal arts college in that all students must also take
21   approximately 60 hours of general education classes from different subject areas. A university **confers**
22   both undergraduate and graduate degrees. Some universities only offer **Master's degrees** in their gradu-
23   ate programs, but others also offer **Doctoral degrees** in different areas of specializations. Not all univer-
24   sities offer the same courses of study or curriculum emphasis, especially in their graduate programs.
25   Some universities are famous for engineering, but others might be famous for business, medicine, or

26   linguistics. It is a good idea to learn more about the university you are thinking about to make sure it
27   offers programs that you are interested in.
28   Another important aspect to take into account when studying in US universities is to explore the
29   opportunities for *practical experiences* beyond the classroom. Many universities offer *internships* that
30   allow students to work in an office or in the field where they can apply the knowledge they learned in the
31   class. An internship is important for students because it provides practical experience. Whatever choices
32   international students make on the type of higher education institutions in the US, they must plan it care-
33   fully and be aware of the outcomes of their educational experience overseas.

Discussion Questions

1. What is the difference between community colleges, liberal arts colleges, and universities?
    a) The purpose or philosophy of the institution
    b) The quality of professors
    c) The size of the community where the institution is located
    d) The kind of teaching, lecture or small group

2. Where can you earn a Master's degree?
    a) A community college
    b) A liberal arts college
    c) A university
    d) All of the above

3. A liberal arts college tries to provide
    a) A specific, practical education
    b) A research-based education
    c) A well-rounded education
    d) A specialized education

4. All universities and colleges in the US follow the same curriculum.
    a) True
    b) False

5. According to the article, what is important when thinking about applying to an institution of higher
    education in the US?
    a) The kinds of degree the institution offers
    b) The opportunities for practical experience
    c) Where it is located
    d) Both a and b

Activity 1: Campus Tour

Goal: Learn about your campus and learn the offices that are important to you as an international student.

Discover your campus: In a small group, take a tour of your college or university campus. Get a campus map and a notebook and write down interesting things you find during your tour. Find the following offices:

▶   Intensive English Program
▶   International Student Office

- ▶ Bursar's Office
- ▶ Registrar's Office
- ▶ Writing Center or Academic Support Center
- ▶ Recreation Center
- ▶ Multicultural Center
- ▶ Counseling Center
- ▶ Information Technology Center
- ▶ Library
- ▶ Student Life and Development
- ▶ Academic Departments, Chairs
- ▶ Dean's Offices

Also, write down any questions you have during your tour. Find the offices that provide support services for international students. What do these offices do? Are there services that you need but the college or university does not have?

Activity 2: Communicating with Professors

E-mailing Professors

Goal: Learn how to e-mail a professor.

E-mail etiquette: The use of e-mail in US colleges and universities is an important part of a student's life. Many professors and instructors prefer to communicate by e-mail to set up appointments and talk about class assignments or other issues. Below are some examples of e-mails. Some are good examples and some are not good examples of acceptable e-mail etiquette. Can you identify which two are good and which two are bad? What do you think might happen to the two students that sent the bad e-mails? How might they revise their e-mails to make them more appropriate? After you are familiar with the format, write an e-mail to your teacher with questions about the syllabus, a class assignment, a grade, or to request an appointment.

Example 1

I wanna meet you about my grade.

Example 2

Dear Dr. Smith,

The purpose of my e-mail is to remind you of our previous meeting on June 2, when you provided an overview of my Graduate Student Research Grant application. During that meeting, you asked me to re-write the proposal and submit it to you for your final approval. That document is attached.

Thank you,

Sarah

Example 3

Dear Dr. Smith, My name is John Smith, and I am a graduate student in your on-line course, ENG 7888: The 19th Century Novel. I have encountered some difficulty with the course and would like to speak with you about ways that I can be successful. I would appreciate your advice and am interested in scheduling an appointment. Please let me know your availability.

Sincerely,

John

Example 4

Hi Professor. I am coming to your office tomorrow to tell you that the grade you gave me in Biology 201 isn't fair and I want you to change it because you didn't think about how hard it is for international students to take a test in only 45 minutes. It's not fair and you need to change the grades and your system.

Marcelo

Activity 3: Interview

Interview an employee in the International Admission Office or the Office of the Registrar in your University

Goal: To get to know the people that work and support university students in your institution.

Prepare some interview questions that you would like to ask to learn more about the office and how it helps international students. Can you think of any other questions?

Sample Questions

1. What is your job in this office?
2. How do you support international students when they come to you?
3. What kinds of things do you do to help international students when they are on campus?
4. Describe your typical day in the office.
5. How do you deal with a difficult situation involving a student?
6. Do you have any questions for me?

Activity 4: Observe a Classroom

Goal: Experience an academic class and learn more about what a typical classroom looks like in the US.

Arrange to visit a university class. Find out what students' majors are and then contact professors in these disciplines. Ask permission for students to attend a class or two for observation. If the IEP class is large, it may be good to find several classes and divide the students into smaller groups of two or three. Have students take notes on what they saw and heard in the classroom. The next class hour, have students report back to the others about their experiences.

Activity 5: Classroom Differences

Goal: *Teach others about the differences between their country's classroom culture and the US classroom culture.*

Develop a compare and contrast presentation in which students demonstrate the differences between classrooms in their countries and those in the United States. Students may even want to role-play this instead of giving a presentation.

> ► Similarities and difference between your education culture and the US
> ► Taboos and faux pas of classroom behavior in your countries and the US
> ► Develop a poster presentation where you clearly show these differences

Activity 6: Student Life Vocabulary

Syllabus/Communication	Academic Calendar	Semester/Quarter	Assignments
Schedule (n)	Course (n)	Semester: 16-week course (n)	Due dates (n)
E-mail/appointments (n)	Registration (n)	Quarter: 10-week course (n)	Group Project (n)
Academic policies (n)	Drop/Add Classes (vp)		Individual Projects (n)
Attendance (n)	Breaks (n)		Homework (n)
Paperwork (n)	Finals (n)		Presentations (n)
Required Textbooks (n)			GPA (n)
Office hours (n)			
Extra Credit (n)			
Student Life		**Athletics**	**Diversity**
Residence Life (n)	Online (n)	Varsity Sports (n)	Multicultural Organizations (n)
Campus Dining (n)	Drop-box (n)	Intramural Sports (n)	International Students Organizations (n)
Health and Well-being (n)	Turn in (v)	Recreation Centers (n)	Culture Shock (n)
Major (n)	Submit (v)	Fitness Center (n)	Adaptation (n)
Minor (n)	Upload (v)		Assimilation (n)
	Sign up (v)		
	Get involved (v)		

With your teacher, study the above vocabulary and learn what these mean on your campus. Can you think of other vocabulary that would be useful?

Chapter 4

Time Is Money

Michael Schwartz

© stanislave/Shutterstock.com

Student Learning Objectives

By the end of this unit, students will be able to:

- ► Appreciate the differences in how time is perceived in their country and the US.
- ► Understand the importance of making appointments.
- ► Understand the importance of keeping appointments.
- ► Make an appointment with a teacher or administrator via e-mail.
- ► Understand the difference between an appointment and a social gathering.

Warm-Up Questions

1. How important is time in your country?
2. When you are invited to a party in your country and the host tells you the party begins at 7:00 p.m., when do people begin to arrive?
3. In what situations is it important to be on time or even early in your country?
4. How is lateness defined or perceived in your country?
5. What do you think the title "Time Is Money" means? What does it tell you about US culture? Do you have a similar expression in your culture?
6. When students need to talk to a teacher in your country, what do they do? How are these meetings arranged? Where do students meet their teachers in your country?
7. Why do you think it's important to make appointments with professors or administrators in the United States?

Take a few minutes to think about the questions above. Write down your answers and then find a partner and share your answers. Do you and your partner come from countries where time is defined differently? How? Do you have expressions in your language and culture to describe time? What are they?

READING 1

Vocabulary

On time
In time
Appointment (n)
Meeting (n, v)
Make an appointment (vp)
Set up (v)
Office hours (np)
Join (v)
Late (adj)

Postpone (v)
Lunchtime (n)
Dinnertime (n)
Schedule (n, v)
Calendar (n)
See you/See somebody (vp)
Hook up (v)[1]
Pencil ___ in (vp)
Drop in (v)

Stop by (v)
Date (n)
Commitment (n)
Talk to (vp)
Get together (vp)
Drop in (n, v)
Talk about (vp)
Get ____ down (vp)

©Dmytro Zinkevych/Shutterstock.com

© Monkey Business Images/Shutterstock.com

---

1 Note: Hook up can also have a different meaning. It can be a request to have casual sex.

Dialogue 1

1	Mahmoud:	*(Walks into Dr. Murphy's office without knocking)* I want to **talk to you** about why my
2		grades are not good.
3	Mr. Murphy:	Okay, and what's your name?
4	Mahmoud:	I'm Mahmoud and my grades are not . . .
5	Mr. Murphy:	Did you make an **appointment**?
6	Mahmoud:	No, but I just want . . .
7	Mr. Murphy:	Uh Mahmoud, it's **lunchtime**. I'm in the middle of my sandwich.
8	Mahmoud:	Yes I know, but my grades are not good because I had to help a friend because he
9		needed to change apartments.
10	Mr. Murphy:	I'd be happy to meet with you, Mahmoud, but can you please **make an appointment**.
11		Here's my card with my e-mail address. Please e-mail me and we can **set up** an
12		appointment to talk. Thank you.

Dialogue 2

13	Sarah:	Hi Cynthia. How's it going?
14	Cynthia:	Good, how about you?
15	Sarah:	I'm fine. Hey, do you want to set up a meeting to talk about our conference presentation?
16	Cynthia:	Ya, I think we need to go over it at least one more time. When can I **stop by**?
17	Sarah:	Let me look at my **calendar**. How about this Thursday at 2:30? Does that work?
18	Cynthia:	No, I'm teaching then. I have class from 2:00 to 2:50 on Thursdays. What about 3:00, right
19		after I get out of class?
20	Sarah:	That works. I'll **pencil you in** for 3:00 this Thursday. E-mail me if something comes up and
21		we need to **postpone** the meeting.
22	Cynthia:	Will do. See you Thursday.
23	Sarah:	Gotta run, I'm **late** for another meeting.

Dialogue 3

24	Ming-su:	What's up Fatma?
25	Fatma:	Not much Ming. What are you doing this Saturday?
26	Ming-su:	Some friends and I are **hooking u**p and going to the movies. Do you want to **join** us?
27	Fatma:	Thanks but I can't. I'm scheduled to go to Chicago tomorrow. I need to go to bed early so
28		I'm **on time** for the flight.
29	Ming-su:	Cool, what are you doing in Chicago?
30	Fatma:	I have to see an advisor at the Turkish consulate to talk about my visa status. I need to know
31		what I have to do if I want to stay and study for my PhD.
32	Ming-su:	Wow! Well good luck with that. **Drop by** when you get back and tell me what you found
33		out. I'm thinking about getting another degree too.

Discussion Questions

1.   What differences do you see in the three dialogues above?
2.   In Dialogue 1, was Mahmoud successful in talking to his professor about his grades in class? Why? What do you think Mahmoud could do to make the conversation go better? What could Mr. Murphy do? How might this interaction go in your country?
3.   In Dialogue 2, what is the relationship between Sarah and Cynthia? Are they friends, colleagues, students, or professors?
4.   What was the purpose of the conversation between Sarah and Cynthia? Were they successful? Why/Why not?
5.   In Dialogue 3, did Fatma and Ming-su make an appointment?
6.   Will Fatma go with Ming-su and his friends to the movies on Saturday night? Why/Why not?
7.   In line 42, Ming-su says, "Drop by when you get back . . ." What does he mean by this?

© alphaspirit/Shutterstock.com

© Monkey Business Images/Shutterstock.com

READING 2

Meetings, Appointments, and Getting Together: What's the Difference?

1   The United States is a culture of meetings. You might say that Americans are "meeting happy," meaning
2   that very little is accomplished unless people get together to talk about an issue and then another meet-
3   ing is scheduled to talk about how the issue was handled or resolved. Why is this important to know and
4   understand? First, if international students want to have a conversation with their professors about
5   grades, attendance, or something else related to school, it's important to make an appointment so that the
6   professor sets aside time to talk. If not, the student may find him or herself in a situation like Mahmoud
7   in Dialogue 1 above. Second, making an appointment is a way of showing respect for people and their
8   time. Third, making appointments also allows everyone going to the meeting to be prepared, so that the
9   meeting is as focused, efficient, and productive as possible. Remember, "Time is money."
10   So what is the difference between a meeting, an appointment, and getting together?
11   A meeting is when people gather to talk about an issue that is related to the organization, such as a
12   school meeting, a business meeting, or even a meeting for a religious organization. These kinds of meet-
13   ings don't just happen spontaneously. Rather, someone will schedule the meeting, make an appointment,
14   and ask others to come to the meeting to talk about issues. Meetings are scheduled by finding a day and
15   time on the calendar when everyone can come together. If you were to look at a professor's or an admin-
16   istrator's calendar, you would see they have many appointments written in their calendars each week.

17 This helps them to be on time and prepared. Meetings can be between people who share the same status,
18 teacher-to-teacher, student-to-student, or between people who have different statuses, supervisor-to-
19 teacher, teacher-to-student. In most cases, meetings tend to be more formal with a specific goal to
20 accomplish. Dialogue 2 above is an example of a typical meeting between two colleagues.

© Sebastian Gauert/Shutterstock.com

21 Getting together is quite different from a meeting or an appointment. Getting together is usually an
22 informal gathering where the purpose is more social than professional. For example, friends might get
23 together on Friday night after a week of work to have a drink, talk about a variety of things, and just relax.
24 Conversations may be about work, family, sports, weather, or other things. Getting together can also be
25 spontaneous, meaning that no previous plan was made to meet. Dialogue 3 above is an example of how
26 people might get together and what they might do.
27 At US universities and colleges, faculty are required to hold "office hours." Office hours are times
28 during the week when the professor is supposed to be in his/her office for the purpose of meeting with
29 students. For example, a professor might list his/her office hours as 3:00 to 5:00 p.m. on Tuesday and
30 Thursday. This means that a student should be able drop in during the posted office hours to talk with
31 the professor. Often times, though, the professor will be talking with another student or involved in
32 another meeting. Thus, if a student really wants to have quality time with a professor, it is advisable to
33 make an appointment.
34 For meeting with a professor or administrator at a US college, it's important to know how to make
35 an appointment. It is also important to keep an appointment once it has been made. Keeping an appoint-
36 ment means going to the meeting at the time that the professor and student agreed on and to not be late
37 or show up at a completely different time and day. Remember, "Time is money."

© Mikheyev Viktor/Shutterstock.com

38   One of the most common ways for students to make an appointment with their professors is to send
39   them an e-mail requesting an appointment. The professor will then respond, agreeing to the appoint-
40   ment with possible times to meet. The student then replies, saying that he or she can come to the profes-
41   sor's office at one of the times the professor lists. If the student cannot come at any of the times the pro-
42   fessor is available, then the two continue to negotiate via e-mail a time when they are both available to
43   meet. See the example e-mail exchange between a student (Monica) and her professor (Dr. Thompson)
44   below:

Monica:

1   Hi Dr. Thompson.
2   I'm Monica. I am in your 9:00 Biology 221 class. I'd like to meet with you to talk about my research
3   paper. When can I come to your office?

Dr. Thompson:

4   Hi Monica.
5   That's fine. I can meet you on Wed. at 10:00 or Thur. at 3:00 p.m. Do either of these times work for
6   you?

Monica:

7   Hi again,
8   I'm sorry but I can't meet at either of those times. I have class at 10:00 on Mon. Wed. and Fri. and I
9   work in the afternoons on Thursdays. Can we meet Friday afternoon?

Dr. Thompson:

10   Hi Monica,
11   Can you meet Friday at 2:00?

Monica:

12   Yes, that's perfect. See you at 2:00 this Friday.
13   Thanks Monica.

Dr. Thompson:

14   Okay Monica. I've got you down for 2:00 this Friday.
15   Have a great day.

Discussion Questions

1. How is the e-mail exchange different from the face-to-face conversation in Dialogue 1?
2. What specific vocabulary does Monica use to make her request? What specific vocabulary does Mahmoud use to make his request? What's the difference?
3. Given the reading "Meetings, Appointments, and Getting Together" what did Monica do that Mahmoud didn't?
4. Can you predict who will have a successful meeting? Why? Why not?
5. Outline the steps that both Monica and Mahmoud took. Where do you think the interaction broke down and where do you think it was successful?

To make an appointment with a professor or administrator, it's important to include the following items:

1. Begin with a polite salutation or introduction.
2. Introduce yourself: tell the person who you are.
3. Ask the person for a meeting.
4. Tell the person why you want to meet or what you want to talk about.
5. Tell the person the days and times you are available to meet or request a meeting during the professor's office hours.
6. End with a polite "thank you."

Activities

Beginning

▶ Information Gap Activity: Have students make up their own schedule for a month. Provide students with a blank calendar for a month. Have students write in times when they are doing something, such as in class, shopping with friends, homework, worship time, tutor appointments, etc. Their calendars should be relatively full, at least 5 to 8 items for each week. These can be imaginary if necessary. Then, pair students and tell them to schedule at least two appointments. The students should not look at each other's calendars. They should negotiate their meeting time orally. Once they identify times they can meet, they should write in their calendars when the meeting will take place.

▶ Caveat: collect the calendars and redistribute them so that students don't have their own calendars. Have them do the activity as described above.

Intermediate/Advanced

▶ Search the Internet for videos on how to make an appointment. Watch at least three of these videos and take notes on the process. What is the same about the processes? What is different? Make your own video in which you are teaching others how to make an appointment to visit a professor at your university.

▶ E-mail: Have your students write an e-mail to you, another teacher, or an administrator to make an appointment. When they have successfully negotiated the appointment, have them print off or take a screen shot of the appointment and bring it to you. Make sure the students keep their appointment. Have them take notes of the appointment and take a picture with the faculty or administrator. Note: they should ask permission to take the picture.

▶ Role-play: Assign students the role of professor, administrator, and student. Have students come to the front of the room and role-play the process of making an appointment.

► Caveat: Have a student just "drop in" unannounced and not during the posted office hours and have the "professor role" deny the student a meeting and then begin the process for making an appointment.

► Have students discuss the difference between making an appointment with a professor and a health care professional. How are these different? How are these the same?

Chapter 5

Logging on, Logging in, and Interfacing: Computing and the Internet in US Universities

Chris DiStasio

© violetkaipa/Shutterstock.com

Student Learning Objectives

By the end of this unit, students will be able to:

► Understand how computer and Internet technology are often used in the US.
► Understand some specific ways university students in the US are often expected to use technology.
► Learn about some free websites that are especially useful for learning English.

Warm-Up Questions

Take a few minutes to think about the questions below. Write down your answers and then share your answers with a partner or small group member.

1. How do people use the Internet in your country?
2. What computer **technology** needs do students have in your country? How are these different or similar to the United States?
3. What is a **learning management system** (LMS)? Have you had experience using an LMS?
4. How do you store computer files? Do you use an online **storage** website, such as Google Drive, Box, or Dropbox?
5. What are some free websites that can help you learn English?
6. What do the computing terms in the title mean? Which two are similar in meaning?
7. What do you think the picture above represents?

© karelnoppe/Shutterstock.com

READING 1

Dialogue 1

1	Lei:	I don't understand why my grade in class is so low.
2	Zeynep:	I know you're a good student . . . there must be some mistake. Did you turn in the book
3		report last week? I know that it was worth a lot of points.
4	Lei:	Book report?
5	Zeynep:	Ya, there was a book report due on Friday.
6	Lei:	How did you know about it?
7	Zeynep:	Do you know the book we've been reading in class?
8	Lei:	Sure.
9	Zeynep:	Professor Jones didn't mention it in class, but he assigned a report on it in our daily
10		homework message. Did you read it?
11	Lei:	Uh, no. I rarely log on to my university e-mail account, and when I do, I usually skim over
12		the homework messages quickly.
13	Zeynep:	Man, you need to get in the habit of checking your university e-mail daily. There's important
14		and useful information that comes across that e-mail, and it's the only e-mail professors use
15		to communicate with their students. You should really read them carefully.
16	Lei:	Ya I know. It's just such a pain logging into all these different websites.

17	Zeynep:	I agree with you but it'll save you from situations like this. I use the daily homework message
18		as a checklist of what I need to do to prepare for the next class and I'm constantly checking
19		the class website for new messages.
20	Lei:	Okay, okay. You made your point.

Related Discussion Questions

1. Why is Lei's grade in the class lower than **expected**?
2. What should Lei do to make sure he does not have the same problem again?
3. What advice does Zeynep give Lei?

© Geo Martinez/Shutterstock.com

Dialogue 2

21	Professor:	Nouran, I need to speak with you about the way you're turning in homework.
22	Nouran:	I'm sorry . . . what's wrong?
23	Professor:	You need to submit your homework using the Blackboard website.
24	Nouran:	I thought it would be fine to send it to you in an e-mail.
25	Professor:	I appreciate that but there's a greater chance of me losing it if you send it by email. Using
26		the Blackboard is a much more organized way to see students' work than through e-mails.
27		More importantly, I can give you a grade directly on the work you submit and then you can
28		see it online quickly.
29	Nouran:	Those are good points. Actually, I've wanted to submit my work on Blackboard, but I
30		haven't been sure how to do it.
31	Professor:	Not a problem. It only takes a few clicks in the right places to submit your work to our class
32		website. Learning management systems can be challenging at first. Professors are usually
33		understanding if there are technical problems, but less so when students don't attempt to
34		learn the system. Can I show you how to submit your homework?
35	Nouran:	Sure. Here is fine. That would be great!

Related Discussion Questions

1. What does the professor need Nouran to do?
2. Why wasn't Nouran submitting her work to the class website?
3. Have you had a similar situation happen to you? How have you handled the situation?

Dialogue 3

36	Carolina:	Here is my homework, professor.
37	Professor:	Thank you, Carolina, but you were supposed to upload your work to D2L rather than give
38		it to me on paper.
39	Carolina:	I know, but I'm not sure how to upload files on D2L.
40	Professor:	It's fine this time, but your work needs to be uploaded to D2L next time in order for you to
41		receive credit for your work. Would you like me to show you how to upload files to D2L?
42	Carolina:	Thanks! That would be really helpful.
43	Professor:	First, do your work in a word processing program like Microsoft Word. Then you save
44		your work in a file on your computer, someplace that's easy for you to remember where
45		it is.
46	Carolina:	Yeah, I know that part.
47	Professor:	(*pointing to the computer screen*) See . . . on D2L when you click on the button that reads
48		"upload," a window comes up. You need to find the file where you saved your work on
49		your computer. When you have found your file, click on it. Finally, click on "open." This
50		should upload your homework, and I'll get it.
51	Carolina:	Thanks! I think I know what to do now.
52	Professor:	Good, let me see you do this.
53	Carolina:	Okay, there's my paper. So I go to D2L, then find the button that says, "upload." Okay, now
54		it's asking me to select a file, so I go to my USB drive and select the file with my paper
55		that's on the USB drive. Then what?
56	Professor:	Click on "submit."
56	Carolina:	Oh, wow! That was simple and it could have saved me $3.00 in printing!
57	Professor:	Awesome. If you have any problems, including problems about technology, you can always
58		send me an e-mail or talk to me during office hours and I'll try to help.

Related Discussion Questions

1. What does the professor need Carolina to do with her assignment?
2. How does the professor help Carolina?
3. What does the professor tell Carolina she should do when she has questions about the university LMS?

© Robert Kneschke/Shutterstock.com

READING 1

Vocabulary

Aspect (n)

Benefit (n)

Essential (adj)

Expect (v)

Commerce (n)

Brick-and-mortar (adj)

Variety (n)

Unless (conj)

Indefinite (adj)

Word processor (n)

Paper (n)

Hard copy (n)

Extensive (adj)

Fluent (adj)

Convenient (adj)

Learning Management System (n)

Application (n)

Hassle (n)

Relay (v)

Post (v)

Verbally (adv)

Efficient (adj)

Keep track of (vp)

Outdated (adj)

Flash drive (n)

Cloud (n)

© Maxx-Studio/Shutterstock.com

© Digital Genetics/Shutterstock.com

The Changing Face of Universities: The Impact of the Internet

1 More and more, computer and Internet technology are not only becoming **aspects** of life that people
2 **benefit** from knowing about, but they are also becoming **essential** tools, and it is **expected** that people
3 know how to use computers and the Internet.

4 People in the United States use computer and Internet technology in many ways, from playing com-
5 puter games to paying bills online. Although a lot of business is still done with paper, more and more
6 **commerce** is done through the Internet. Indeed, doing business online can be more effective and **effi-**
7 **cient** than doing business in a **brick-and-mortar** location. For example, through Amazon (<u>www.</u>
8 <u>amazon.com</u>), you can purchase a wide **variety** of items that are sent directly to you. Sites such as Ama-
9 zon allow you to buy just about anything you could obtain in a brick-and-mortar store, but without ever
10 having to leave your home. Such sites also let you get a lot of things you would not be able to find in a
11 local store.

12 In universities in the United States, students are expected to use computer and Internet technology
13 in a variety of ways. First of all, students are expected to use computers for untimed writing assignments.
14 This includes essays, various kinds of reports, and research **papers** to be turned in at a specific time and
15 date. **Unless** you are planning on staying in the United States for an **indefinite** period of time, it is prob-
16 ably best to buy a laptop, netbook, or tablet so that you can do your homework and complete your assign-
17 ments. Students are expected to use a **word processor,** such as Microsoft Word, to write assignments or
18 give presentations using Powerpoint. It is becoming more and more common for papers to be submitted
19 electronically rather than as **hard copies.** Most professors prefer that the assignments be submitted via
20 the **learning management system** their university uses. If the professor requires hard copies of assign-
21 ments, then students can usually print the assignments out at the university library or a local public
22 library for a small cost. It is a good idea for a student to purchase an inexpensive printer when coming
23 to the United States for **extensive** study. It can be much less of a **hassle** to use a printer at home because
24 it is more **convenient** to print at home, and it is **ultimately** cheaper.

© Sarunyu_foto/Shutterstock.com

25 Another way university students are often required to use technology is through a learning manage-
26 ment system (LMS), such as Blackboard, D2L, or Moodle. An LMS is a software or Internet-based **appli-**
27 **cation** under which websites for individual university classes are set up. If your instructor uses a class
28 website that is part of an LMS, you should consider yourself **fortunate** because it is a **convenient** way to
29 view and submit information related to classes, and it is a great way to become more **fluent** in using com-

30   puter and Internet technology. Through a class website that is part of an LMS, instructors can **relay**
31   important information to students, such as messages and assignment files, in a convenient and carefully
32   organized way. The instructor simply **posts** a message explaining assignments and possibly includes file
33   attachments related to the message. Students are required to read and understand the message written on
34   the class website and follow the assignment as directed in it. It is important to know that the written mes-
35   sage will likely have information in it that was not discussed **verbally** in class (see Dialogue 1 above). If
36   your instructor uses an LMS, it is very important for you to check the class website on a daily basis and
37   become familiar with what is on the website and how to navigate the different parts so that you can check
38   messages, view the calendar, find drop boxes, and enter discussion rooms when you need to. By learning
39   how to use the LMS effectively and efficiently, you will be more prepared for your university classes. If
40   students do not pay enough attention to messages and other assignment information in their class web-
41   sites, their performance and grades may suffer. Submitting assignments through a class website is often
42   considered more efficient than doing the work on paper. Finally, a class website can also allow instructors
43   to **keep track of** students' grades and in some cases help students track their grades themselves.

© Maxx-Studio/Shutterstock.com

44   Most university libraries now have extensive websites containing multiple resources. Students can
45   look up information about books, journal articles, newspaper and magazine articles, and other kinds of
46   resources. University libraries are often connected to online databases that have a wide variety of articles
47   for students and faculty to use for research and for doing class assignments. Although students may need
48   to visit the university library physically to check out a book, students can often access articles directly on
49   the library website from their apartment. Also, if a student has questions about a resource or can't find a
50   particular article, most library websites have an online chat option where students can communicate
51   online with a librarian.

© Nucleartist/Shutterstock.com

52   Although it is not necessarily a requirement, everyone, especially students, may find it much easier
53   to store and keep track of important computer files, especially assignment-related files, in one place. Stu-
54   dents may find it convenient to store these files on a **flash drive** (USB drive), but storing the files through
55   **cloud**-based tools such as Google (Google Drive), Box, and Dropbox is becoming more and more popu-
56   lar. One reason is that these cloud-based tools can be synced to multiple devices and can be accessed
57   anywhere, so there's no physical device that could be forgotten, lost, or broken. These cloud-based tools
58   usually give users a **generous** amount of free storage space. If more space is needed, then it's possible to
59   buy more. Thus, it is now possible to be working on a project in the library with some friends, then go
60   home and get on the home computer or tablet, log on to the cloud, and continue working on the same
61   project.
62   Every new generation has had to learn new technologies for the world they live in. At one time, the
63   "pencil" was considered new technology and it took people time to learn how to use the pencil effectively.
64   The same is true for computers and the Internet. Today, technology is changing at remarkable rates and
65   it is bringing the world closer together. It is now possible to learn a foreign language, to buy clothes, or
66   to earn a college degree completely online from nearly anywhere in the world. This was not possible fif-
67   teen years ago. All you need is a computer and an Internet connection. In fact, technology is changing so
68   fast that this chapter may be **outdated** before it is even published!

Reading Comprehension

1. List some specific ways people use the Internet.
   a)
   b)
   c)

2. List some examples of ways students use computer and Internet technology. How many of these are school-related and how many are for social purposes?
   a)
   b)
   c)

3. Why is it a good idea to purchase a printer when you are a student?
   a) To save money
   b) For convenience
   c) To make doing homework easier
   d) Both a & b

4. Describe how instructors use **learning management systems (LMS)**?

5. List some ways that students are expected to use LMS's?

6. List some ways that online library resources can be helpful.

7. What are some **benefits** of using the **cloud**?

Vocabulary Exercise

1. What is a synonym for *aspect* as it is used in line 1?
   a) Part
   b) Important
   c) Necessary
   d) Computer

2. What is the difference between an *online store* and a *brick-and-mortar* store in line 7?

3. Name something that is **efficient** (line 6)? Describe how it's efficient?

4. What does indefinite (line 15) mean?
   a) No time
   b) No plan
   c) No end
   d) No homework

5. What is the opposite of *convenient* as it is used in line 28?
   a) Efficient
   b) Extensive
   c) Hassle
   d) Advantage

6. Describe how someone can become more *fluent* with computers (line 29).

7. What are some ways to communicate other than **verbally** (line 35)?

8. What's another way to say *keep track of* (line 43)?
   a) Follow
   b) Organize
   c) Drive
   d) None of the above

9. Give an example of a *cloud*-based tool (line 55).

10. Which of the following technologies have become *outdated* (line 68)? Choose all that apply. Can you think of other technologies that have become outdated?
    a) The typewriter
    b) The scanner
    c) The television
    d) The bicycle

Suggested Activities

Any level

▶ (For teachers, specifically: Even if your program, school, college, or university does not provide a learning management system (LMS), there are many options for having one for your classes, such as www.schoology.com, www.latitudelearning.com, and www.coursesites.com, which are free (with more features available in paid subscriptions). Although Google Drive (www.drive.google.com) is not as well known as an LMS, Google Drive in connection with its very useful individual functions (Presentation, Document, Spreadsheet, Form, and Draw) can serve as a very flexible, efficient LMS).

▶ Make a Quizlet of vocabulary covered in your class at www.quizlet.com. Quizlet makes practice with class sets of vocabulary convenient, useful, and enjoyable with digital flashcards, games (such as a traditional matching game), tests, and spoken vocabulary and definitions. https://www.youtube.com/watch?v=O4yneplozIY. Before you make a Quizlet from vocabulary featured in a textbook or based on a particular topic, it may be a good idea to search on Quizlet for related sets of vocabulary. It's possible a Quizlet vocabulary activity has already been made.

▶ Make an Excel spreadsheet or a Google Spreadsheet (through Google Drive) to help you track a skill you need to develop on your own. (For teachers, specifically: Making Google Spreadsheets for individual students and then sharing the spreadsheets with the individual students is a good way to track students' progress on a variety of skills.) Here are some suggestions for skills students at different levels can develop on their own and keep track of through a spreadsheet:

- ○ (All levels) Different levels of mastery at specific grammar skills, perhaps based on specific related exercises that students can complete and test themselves on at their own pace
- ○ (All levels) Learning to touch type with an American English keyboard, along with very useful typing exercise and training websites such as www.typingweb.com
- ○ (Intermediate/advanced) Developing greater reading speed, along with the free online tool www.spreeder.com and readings found online (preferably readings with reading comprehension questions), such as readings at www.cdlponline.org.

Beginning

▶ Do an Internet scavenger hunt! Find the following information by doing a web search. Ask your instructor for help finding the right keywords to use in a web search. Then present the information to the class on your own, or with a partner or in a small group:

1. The population of your home town
2. The population of the United States
3. Famous people from your home town
4. Famous people from the town/city in the United States you are living in
5. A fun place in the town/city in the United States you are living in
6. A historical place in the town/city in the United States you are living in

Note: You can make a simple presentation with tools such as Microsoft PowerPoint, Google Presentation (www.drive.google.com), or Prezi (www.prezi.com) to make the presentation more interesting.

▶ Search for a fun website or web exercise related to an area of English you are having difficulty with. Just type in the word/words for what you are having difficulty with (for example, *pronunciation* or *irregular verbs*) and then type *exercise*. Skim the entries that come up to find an exercise that seems interesting. Do the exercise and then report on the website you found in a presentation. During the presentation, show your audience the steps it takes to get to the exercise then show how to use the exercise. This activity is especially useful as a process presentation assignment.

Note: You can use applications and online tools such as Microsoft PowerPoint, Google Presentation (www. drive.google.com), or Prezi (www.prezi.com) to make the presentation more interesting.

Intermediate/advanced

▶ Make a group presentation using www.voicethread.com. With VoiceThread, students record their comments through audio or video about an image, a video, or even a piece of writing posted by the teacher or by students who are making VoiceThreads themselves. The comments can then be seen by all who have access to the VoiceThread. Because everyone has access to the same VoiceThread, the teacher and/or students can develop an interactive, multimedia, multi-skills conversation both in class and outside of class. You can present the VoiceThread with other group members in front of the class.

▶ Improve any writing assignment! The tools www.wordandphrase.info and COCA (the Corpus of Contemporary American English) at http://corpus.byu.edu/coca/ can help you improve your writing greatly in the following ways:

1. Help you find out how academic your writing is and increase the level of academic vocabulary in your writing.
2. Make your writing more fluent by locating collocations for the vocabulary you use.
3. Help you easily find the most commonly used synonyms (often better and more accurately than a thesaurus can) to do the following:

   ○ Improve the quality of any writing through using a greater variety of synonyms
   ○ Use your own words in summaries more easily

Here is a step-by-step guide for using the online tools mentioned above: http://tinyurl.com/lzpour5

▶ Make your own website. Put your writing from class on the website and add photos and videos that relate to your writing. There are many sites on which you can create your own website for free (with a greater variety of functions for a paid subscription), such as www.weebly.com, www.wordpress.com, or www.sites.google.com. Your class could make its own website, too!

▶ Make your own literary magazine, for your own writing or the writing of your small group members or entire class. There are several websites such as www.issuu.com and www.joomag.com that can help you make a digital magazine easily.

▶ Start an online book club for your small group or entire class. In an online book club, students read books that may or may not be assigned in class, either the same book together or different books. Students discuss what they like about the books they are reading and even post photographs online. If there is no time in class for discussing the books, a variety of forms of online communication can enable conversation, from discussion forums available through the class's learning management system and posts on free blogs, such as www.blogger.com and www.wordpress.com, to social networking sites, such as Facebook.

▶ Make a collaborative writing on a Google Document with a group of students or the whole class. For example, students can make a story or essay together, each student providing his or her own sentence, one student after another, until the story or essay is finished. The project can be done in class or outside of class on separate computers because all students will have access to a single, shared document. Furthermore, students can help each other edit the story and make side comments on the story in the Google Document. Here are step-by-step directions on how to make a Google Document and use other Google Drive functions: https://docs.google.com/document/d/1XaIWU8LiYiEd9vdKzcuTjC7 W2H_F83GJZEGISMqEWn0/edit?usp=sharing

▶ Another useful activity involving group writing, editing, and discussion (through side comments) in a Google Document is for a small group or class of students to write a story or essay with vocabulary featured in class and edit it together. Also, students can write and edit example sentences or paragraphs focusing on a particular skill with grammar, punctuation, and/or vocabulary.

Chapter 6

Hit the Books: Grades and Academic Expectations in the US

Moussa Traore

© Alan Poulson Photography/Shutterstock.com

© Photographee.eu/Shutterstock.com

Student Learning Objectives

By the end of this unit, students will be able to:

- ► Describe the differences in grading between school systems in their country and the US.
- ► Understand the differences in faculty expectations for earning grades.
- ► Understand grade policies and grade politics in the US.
- ► Determine why final grades might appear different from what they expected.

Warm-Up Questions

1. Are grades important in your country? If so, how important are they?
2. What are student grades mostly based on: knowledge of subject matter, or on things you did, such as writing papers, group participation, and attendance?
3. Is it easy or hard to get a passing grade in your country? Why?
4. How are final grades given in your country: letters (A, B, C) or numbers (5, 4, 3) or some other way? Can you think of why?
5. Does the educational system in your country have an honor or distinction system at the end of the school year?
6. How seriously do students care or worry about their grades during the school year?
7. When do students get their grades in your country?
8. Can students skip a quarter or semester without losing out on the whole year?
9. What happens if students earn failing grades?
10. What would happen if a student's final grades or transcript contained a mistake?
11. What do you think the title of this chapter means?

Think for a while about these questions and write your answers down. Then find a classmate and share your answers. Make sure you discuss and come up with what is similar among your two experiences, and what is different. Why do you think there might be differences?

DIALOGUE 1

Vocabulary

well enough (adv. p)	even though (adv. p)	bitter (adj.)
improve (v.)	as close as (adj.)	warned (adj.)
succeed (v.)	normally (adv.)	intimidated (adj.)
ambitious (adj.)	generally (adv.)	courage (n.)
perfect (adj.)	passing (adj.)	lose (v.)
honors (n.)	failed (v.)	throughout (adv.)
positive (adj.)	smarter (adj.)	used to (v p)
astonishment (n.)	worse (adv.)	safe (adj.)
catch up (v p)	discouraged (adj.)	ride (n.)
sweat it (v p)	crushed (adj.)	

Read the following dialogue carefully; then answer the discussion questions.

Dialogue 1

1	Jonas:	Hey Joe; how'd you do?
2	Joe:	Oh. On the test? I did **well *enough***. Not great, but well enough.
3	Jonas:	Really? How so? Even *I* did well.
4	Joe:	Great to hear; I told you that you can **improve** and **succeed** quickly.
5	Jonas:	What'd you get?
6	Joe:	80% , a low B. It's only the first quiz though. I can improve.
7	Jonas:	You must be very **ambitious**. 80% is like 16 out of 20, which gets you **honors**! Do you want to
8		be **perfect**?
9	Joe:	Are you kidding? It's only a low B; to get honors you need an A+.
10	Jonas:	(*with **astonishment***) Then what did I get? A 69%, which is . . . I think . . . I thought is almost
11		14 out of 20, which is good. In my country this is considered a good grade. Passing. Are you
12		telling me that this is a bad grade here? What am I supposed to get?
13	Joe:	You can **catch up**. Don't **sweat it**; it's only the first quiz.
14	Jonas:	So, I didn't do well. I didn't do well at all, **even though** I worked hard. What does 69% mean
15		then?
16	Joe:	It's a D+. It's **as close** to a C- **as** possible. A C is **normally** the **passing** grade.
17	Jonas:	So, I **failed**. Now I see that I don't know as much as I thought.
18	Joe:	You worked hard; it's true. You will learn to work **smarter**.
19	Jonas:	Oh, I see. That happened to you.
20	Joe:	I did much **worse** on my first quiz and was **discouraged**, **crashed**, and **bitter**.
21	Jonas:	I am sorry to hear that, but now I know.
22	Joe:	That's the spirit. You'll catch up **throughout** the semester.
23	Jonas:	I need to; I have to. I am not **used to** failing. . . Ah, the bus is here . . . See you later.
24	Joe:	See you later man. Have a **safe ride**.

Discussion Questions

1. Who did better on the test, Jonas or Joe?
2. What did Joe know that Jonas didn't know about the grading system?
3. How differently do Jonas and Joe handle failure (on a test)?
4. How would you have reacted if you were Jonas?
5. Was Joe a good, helpful friend? Explain why.

Choose the appropriate word or expression for each sentence from the table below. Note there are more words in the table than you need and there may be more than one correct answer for some sentences.

fail	generally	positive
bitter	discouraged	catch up
succeed	warned	lose
perfect	bitter	Sweat it
improve	honors	even though
astonished	safe	intimidated
as close as	ambitious	

1. After working so hard for my test and not passing it, I felt _____ and _____.

2. But when I worked hard to _____ on what I did not know, I did very well on the following test; in fact, I was _____ that my grade was even good enough for _____!

3. So if I do not do well on a test now, I will not _____; I will only work harder.

4. My friend was able to _____ his grade from C to B–, but he needs to be more _____; he needs to think of getting a B+, A–, or even a _____ score.

5. If you miss the last bus of the day, you will have to ask someone for a _____ ride home. In this town, people are _____ kind (nice).

6. In order to not _____ points because I missed a quiz, I need to go to every class the rest of the semester.

7. I can't believe I got a D– on the last test. The professor _____ that the test would be difficult but this is crazy.

8. The teacher told me that _____ I had a good grade on the first two tests, I may still not _____ in the course if I do poorly on the next tests.

DIALOGUE 2

Vocabulary

remember (v.)	material (n.)	untamed (adj.)
based on (v p)	maximise (v.)	behavior (n.)
sets (n.)	chances (n.)	serious (adj.)
bother (v.)	score (n.)	current (adj.)
keep in mind (v p)	ticked off (v p)	counts (v.)
ace (v.)	ignored (adj.)	day 1 (np)
multiple-choice (n.)	overlooked (adj.)	necessarily (adv.)
fill-in-the-blanks (np)	tardiness (n.)	priorities (n.)
compose (v.)	shoddy (adj.)	managing (v.)
memorization (n.)	overall (adj.)	either (pron.)

Please read the following dialogue and answer the discussion questions.

Dialogue 2

1   Debby: Hi Aï; ready for this one?
2   Aïcha: Hi Deb; what are you saying?
3   Debby: Don't you **remember** we have a test **based on** the last **sets** of homework?
4   Aïcha: We're still far from the final; I won't **bother** much.
5   Debby: **Keep in mind** that we did not **ace** even the last small, **multiple-choice** and **fill-in-the-blanks**
6   test questions; this time, we will even have to **compose** a few paragraphs with the new words.
7   Aïcha: I am good at **memorization**. When the final test comes close, I will learn the **material** and
8   **maximize** my **chances** of getting a perfect **score**, and a good, **passing** grade.
9   Debby: (*Ticked off*) By then you've failed! The grade on the final does not replace all the poor tests and
10   quizzes, **ignored** or **overlooked** homework, missed classes, late arrivals or **tardiness**, **shoddy**
11   participation, and **overall untamed behavior** as a student.
12   Aïcha: Why are you getting so **serious**?
13   Debby: You will look even more serious if you check your **current** grade and your **chances** of passing.
14   Everything **counts** from **day 1**. The final is only another test, not **necessarily** more important
15   than the others.
16   Aïcha: I've got to have some fun though. I can't follow all that all semester.
17   Debby: It's called **priorities**. Make them work together by **managing** your time for **either**.

Discussion Questions

1. Was Debby happy with Aïcha? Why?
2. What is the most important thing that Aïcha is mistaken about?
3. If you were Aïcha, how would you continue the exchange?
4. What do you think that Debby will do in order to ensure that she gets better grades?
5. How is Aïcha (Dialogue 2) different from Jonas (Dialogue 1)?

Choose the most appropriate word for each situation.

1. _____ is when you come late to class.
    a) Material
    b) Chances
    c) Tardiness
    d) Day 1

2. If you can everything that was said in class last week, you are good at _____.
    a) behavior
    b) memorization
    c) ignored
    d) remember

3. Her cousin told her: "_____ that you need to study in order to succeed."
    a) score
    b) multiple choice
    c) keep in mind
    d) priorities

4. The teacher said that each homework assignment _____, so we have to do all assignments.
    a) current
    b) untamed
    c) shoddy
    d) counts

5. Only the very best students, or those who have studied very well, can _____ a test.
    a) sets
    b) overall
    c) ace
    d) score

6. To _____ is to write sentences or a text, not just a list of words.
    a) bother
    b) maximize
    c) compose
    d) either

7. My roommate was not happy at all; she was _____ by the neighbor's comments about her behavior.
    a) ignored
    b) ticked off
    c) serious
    d) fill-in the blanks

8. I am sorry to tell you that _____ your grades, you cannot pass to the next level.
    a) managing
    b) necessarily
    c) based on
    d) maximize

9. Your _____ grade shows that you know the material that we have seen from day 1.
   a) shoddy
   b) maximize
   c) current
   d) overlooked

10. It is not _____ true that a good grade on the final test will make you pass the class.
    a) counts
    b) based on
    c) necessarily
    d) overall

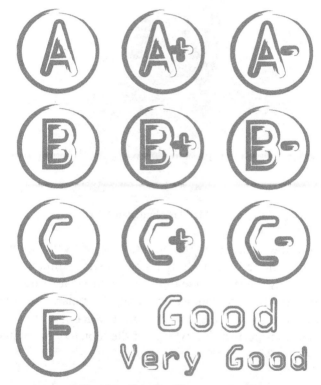

© Phanthip Chittabut/Shutterstock.com

READING 1

Grades and Expectations: Different Countries, Different Systems, Different Practices

1   Unlike many other countries or school systems that give grades in numbers, in the US, grades are based
2   on letters (A–F or U/S). At the end of a semester, these letters will appear on the student's transcript. In
3   the other systems, the final grades can be out of 20, 10, or on another number.

© Maridav/Shutterstock.com

4   What is important to know is that the grading rationale and value interpretation are also different.
5   One could say that in the US there is an underlying optimistic assumption of students' ability to reach
6   "perfection," (i.e., full knowledge of the course topic and to prove it through homework, tests, and proj-
7   ects). It is interesting to know that, of course, tests and other class activities are made based on that
8   assumption so that students can score as high. In systems in other countries where the exact number over
9   20 is given, 20/20 is seen as the "perfect" knowledge of the topic/course material.

©Raymond Gregory/Shutterstock.com

10   Comparing grading systems from other countries to the US system is like comparing apples to
11   oranges. In other grading systems in the world, the assumption is that achieving perfection is only for
12   geniuses. Thus, achieving 50% or a little higher is considered not only passing, but being good. That is
13   why in the US you can get 90% on a test, or even 97%, and earn an A saying that you've come as close to
14   full knowledge as possible. In systems such as the ones Jonas and Aïcha come from (where exact numbers

15 count), a 90% is virtually out of the question (except for very exact sciences such as mathematics or cal-
16 culus), students will have passed if they succeed at 50%.
17   The requirements in terms of work are much different from that of the 50% in the US (knowing that
18 50% in the US is a clear fail and is not a target of anyone). So, the 50% in Jonas' and Aïcha's systems is
19 often as hard to get as the 70% in the US, yet they both mean the same thing in their countries: passing.
20 Because of this difference, Jonas was confused about getting almost 70% while aware that his level is not
21 good yet. So he might first have thought of how easy it is to get not only a passing grade, but a good one;
22 then he found out that that grade did reflect his level, except that it appeared inflated. Once he is
23 reminded about the difference and given an explanation of how it works, he was set to deal with it better.
24   Aïcha's case is, similarly, an assumption that the system in her country and that in the US are the
25 same, when in fact, they are quite different. In many systems, especially after high school, rigorous appli-
26 cation of class rules such as regular attendance is not applied; not that it is not encouraged, but students
27 are seen as responsible, adult enough to know what to do—whether that is true for all of them or not.

©Vixit /Shutterstock.com

28   But the important thing in the above dialogues is that Aïcha is still thinking that she can go by that
29 option and succeed in the US. In her system, the final exam counts more; and, most often, a national test
30 determines if someone goes to the next level or not, thus, transcripts of earlier levels matter less. For no
31 matter what your transcript, if you didn't pass the national test, you don't move up. Hence, the focus is
32 more on the national test than class exams for some students. In the US, there is no such national exam
33 structure; and every transcript counts, regardless of level as they are requested when applying to schools
34 and even jobs.
35   These are but a few, yet key, examples of how ignoring cultures in educational practice can set you
36 up for complications. Consider the next dialogue.

© wavebreakmedia/Shutterstock.com

DIALOGUE 3
Vocabulary

turn a new leaf (vp)   care (n.)
potential (adj.)   progress (n.)
focus (n.)

Please read the following dialogue and answer the discussion questions.

Dialogue 3

1	Ms. Randal:	Good morning Usman.
2	Usman:	Good morning Ms. Randal. I am happy to see you.
3	Ms. Randal:	Good to know. I am happy to see you too. And I am even more . . . happy, or
4		happier, to see that you seem to be doing well with school in general.
5	Usman:	Yes . . . I've **turned a new leaf**, studying hard, and I am passing all my classes.
6	Ms. Randal:	You are! How about that for a good day! I thought . . . you had the **potential** and
7		only needed more **focus** and **care**.
8	Usman:	Yea. Yea. I didn't know that my grades was . . . my grades were going to become so bad.
9	Ms. Randal:	They sure could have kept going that way.
10	Usman:	Then mid-term was *not* good.
11	Ms. Randal:	. . .
12	Usman:	After the mid-term I asked questions and heard people and thought "I need to make
13		some changes. So, I started going to class, doing homework, asking for help, and
14		following my **progress**. I think the change was good.
15		Now I am fine and happy.
16	Ms. Randal:	*I* see.
17	Usman:	Thank you.

Discussion Questions

1. How is this exchange (Dialogue 3) different from Dialogue 1 and Dialogue 2?
2. How is Usman similar to Jonas?
3. How is Usman similar to Aïcha?
4. What could be reasons why Usman started poorly?
5. Who is Ms. Randal? Guess her role. What might she have done to, or for, Usman?

Write the correct words in the appropriate blanks.

Turn a new leaf   Focus   Progress
Potential   Care

Jonathan, if you want to pass this class you're going to have to _____ and begin studying for the

exams and participating in the group work. You have the _____ to be an excellent student, but I get

the impression that you don't _____. If you _____ and make _____ over the

next couple of months, then you might be able to pass this class.

Activities (for all levels)

1. Continue the exchange between Joe and Jonas (assuming you have five to ten minutes before the bus comes).

2. Creatively expand Debby's and Aïcha's conversation.

3. Elaborate on Usman's and Ms. Randal's chat.

4. Imagine and act out a conversation between Ms. Randal and Aïcha.

5. Create a dialogue between Jonas and Debby.

6. Acting as Joe and Aïcha, have a chat in front of the library.

7. You (**A**) are the teacher, counselor, or advisor of an international student in the US. The student has a variety of challenges (related to class expectations and grades) and comes to you for advice. (**B**) Create typical challenges and take them to (**A**) for advice. Act it out.

8. Invite some former IEP students to class and ask them to talk about their experiences in their university classes. What kinds of expectations did the teachers have? How were these different than their experiences in the IEP and in their home country?

9. Invite an academic advisor to class and ask the advisor to talk about the expectations that faculty have for students. Have the advisor explain the grading system in the US and have students then discuss how the systems are different.

10. Have students bring in their transcripts from their home country. One transcript should be the one they received from school. The other transcript should be one that has been calibrated to the US system. Have them compare and then discuss the differences. What did they think about the grade they received initially? What do they think now by a US standard?

11. Have students create a skit that they can present for the entire IEP or during an orientation.

For More Advanced Levels

1. A kind and friendly teacher (**C**) just turned the grades in, and you (**D**) have failed his or her class. Given that the teacher is approachable, you go to him or her to express your surprise, citing by the way all the great instances where you were convinced that you would not fail.

   You (**C**) are the kind and friendly teacher who has the records and all the details explaining the failing final grade. Professionally and, still, kindly explain to the student (**D**) how the result is the product of performance, not one of perceptions related to friendliness. You (**C**) might hint that the friendliness was actually part of encouraging ways for students to learn and succeed, not the opposite.

2. Write a three-paragraph text giving advice to international students (from a place you know) about bad habits to avoid once they come to study in the US.

3. Write a 5-paragraph essay on anything you have ever seen, experienced, or heard about how cultural differences have influenced students' perceptions of grades or academic expectations.

4. Watch the following YouTube video. Then have students research one of the countries and give a presentation about its educational system. Also, students can critique the video's criteria for selection. https://www.youtube.com/watch?v=CtG70v550Y0

5. Before watching the video, have students brainstorm together what it takes to be happy and healthy. Ask students to make a list of the things they discussed. Next, watch the following YouTube video. What according to this video are the keys to being happy and healthy? How can getting an education improve or decrease the chances of achieving happiness and health? Ask students to make their own presentation, even post it on YouTube, of what they believe it takes to be happy and healthy. https://www.youtube.com/watch?v=46La-hV_PLs

6. Watch portions of the following Ted Talks: Discuss these people's views of education. What values or expectations are expressed?
   a) https://www.youtube.com/watch?v=dilnw_dP3xk
   b) https://www.youtube.com/watch?v=46La-hV_PLs

See No Evil, Hear No Evil, Speak No Evil: Negotiating Social Taboos in a Second Language Environment

Laura Code

© Velazquez77/Shutterstock.com

Student Learning Objectives

By the end of this unit, students will be able to:

▶ Define the term "taboo."

▶ Identify and discuss similarities and differences between their first and second language culture social taboos.

▶ Examine why certain second language behaviors are problematic for them.

▶ Understand what topics may be taboo in American culture and how these topics differ in the first culture.

▶ Write about how they handle cultural differences in their daily interactions.

Warm-Up Questions

1. What does the word "taboo" mean to you?
2. Are there behaviors that are socially taboo in your home country? Are these taboos cultural or religious? Do you agree or disagree with these taboos?
3. Are there American cultural behaviors that are problematic for you?
4. How do you react when you encounter a behavior that is socially taboo to you?
5. Is your reaction different if the behavior is from someone in your own cultural group? From outside your cultural group? Why?
6. Are you familiar with the expression in the title? Do you have a similar expression in your language?

Take a few minutes to think about the questions above. Write down your answers. Make a list of some taboos from your country. Next, make a list of American cultural behaviors that are problematic for you. Compare and discuss your lists with a partner. Are there similarities between your lists and your partner's? What are they? Are there differences? What are they?

READING 1

Vocabulary

garage sale (n)	rude (adj)	socially inappropriate (adj)
browse (v)	to complicate matters (vp)	sensitive (adj)
personal (adj)	torn (v)	burdensome (adj)
inappropriateness (n)	intrusive (adj)	cultural difference (n)
uncomfortable (adj)	pry (v)	open (adj)
taboo (n)	private (adj)	cultural standards (n)
cultural expectation (n)	flustered (v)	navigate (v)

© Alan Gleichman/Shutterstock.com

Mind Your Own Business: Janette's Day at a Garage Sale

1   Recently, I (Janette) went to a **garage sale** in my new neighborhood. While I was **browsing**, the woman
2   having the sale greeted me. She seemed nice and we chatted about the things she was selling. She told me
3   that many items had belonged to her children who were no longer living at home.
4   "Do you have kids?" she asked.
5   "No," I said lightly. "I don't."
6   "Well, why not?" she said with a grin.
7   I tried to keep the surprised look off of my face. I knew that Americans often ask questions of strang-
8   ers, but I wasn't expecting something so **personal**. I was amazed by her **inappropriateness**. I had
9   responded to her first question. Why should I have to explain myself to her? She didn't even know me!
10   "I just don't want to be a mom," I said quietly, trying to keep the anger from my voice. I could feel
11   my face getting hot, so I turned and pretended to inspect a dish on a nearby table. I was **uncomfortable**
12   and wanted her to stop asking me questions. In fact, I wanted her to leave me alone.
13   "Kids are great," she continued. "You'd be a great mom, don't you think?"
14   "Mind your own business, lady," I thought to myself. But I knew I was trapped. Even though her
15   questions were **taboo** to me, I recognized there was an American **cultural expectation** to answer her. I
16   didn't want to reply, but I also did not want her to think people from my country were **rude**. To further
17   **complicate matters**, my culture requires young people to answer questions from elders. I was really **torn**
18   about what to do.

© haeryung stock images/Shutterstock.com

19   I smiled weakly and said, "Maybe." Glancing at my watch, I said, "Oh! Look at the time. I must go.
20   Goodbye!" And with that, I walked briskly to my car. I couldn't get away from her fast enough. What an
21   **intrusive** person!
22   When I got to my car, I could feel my heart racing. I was angry with the woman for **prying** into my
23   **private** life. I was frustrated that she had made me feel so **flustered** and unable to stand up for myself. I
24   don't understand why some people think it's okay to ask strangers personal questions. I think it is **socially**
25   **inappropriate**.
26   In my culture, you would only ask a relative or close friend such a **sensitive** question. Sometimes you
27   wouldn't even ask such questions of a relative or friend. Certain topics are too personal. If a stranger
28   wants to share personal information with me, that is his or her decision. But even then, I really don't want
29   people to share such things. It can feel **burdensome**. Plus, I am often confused about how to respond. In
30   my culture, people are usually pretty private and don't share personal information. This is a big **cultural**
31   **difference** between my home country and the US. Most of the time, I try to be **open**, recognizing that
32   different **cultural standards** exist. It can be hard **navigating** these differences, though.

33   I've been thinking of ways to handle situations like this in the future. A possible solution is to politely
34   say, "I'm not comfortable discussing this topic." Next time I'm in a similar situation, I'm going to say this
35   and see what happens. It may be hard for me to do this, but I think I'll be more comfortable doing this
36   than sharing personal details of my life with strangers.

Discussion Questions

1. How do you define *taboo*?
2. Do you think the writer handled the situation well? If so, what did she do well? If not, how would you have handled it differently?
3. How do you react when you encounter American behaviors that are taboo in your first culture?
4. Has your attitude toward certain taboo behaviors changed since living in the US? If so, how has it changed? If not, why hasn't it changed?
5. Have you experienced a situation like the one in the story? What happened? How did you react? If you had that experience today, would your reaction be different? Why or why not?
6. In line 34, Janette says she's going to say "I'm not comfortable discussing this topic" the next time she's asked a personal question. What other strategies or expressions might you use to remove yourself from the conversation? Can you role play this situation in class?

Comprehension/Vocabulary

1. What is the main idea of this essay?
   a) Culture differences can arise any time.
   b) It is important to be prepared for culture differences.
   c) Cultural differences are no big deal.
   d) All of the above.

2. Why was Janette **flustered** in line 23?
   a) She couldn't buy what she wanted.
   b) She didn't want to answer personal questions from a stranger.
   c) She wanted to ask the woman personal questions.
   d) She didn't know what a garage sale was.

3. What does **torn** in line 17 mean in this story?
   a) Ripped
   b) Broken
   c) Uncertain
   d) Confident

4. How does Janette respond to the woman's first question (line 4)?
   a) She tells the woman to mind her own business.
   b) She smiles and doesn't say anything.
   c) She gets in her car and leaves.
   d) She says she doesn't have kids.

5. How does Janette respond to the woman's second question (line 6)?
    a) She gets in her car and leaves.
    b) She says she doesn't want to be a mom.
    c) She shares more information about her personal life.
    d) She asks why the woman wants to know.

6. How does Janette respond to the woman's third question (line 13)?
    a) She looks at her watch and leaves.
    b) She doesn't say anything.
    c) She tells the woman to mind her own business.
    d) She answers, then looks at her watch and leaves.

7. Why does Janette answer the woman's questions?
    a) She knows she is expected to answer.
    b) She doesn't want to appear rude.
    c) She likes to share personal information.
    d) Both a & b

8. How does Janette plan to deal with future situations like the one she described?
    a) She will adopt a more open attitude toward personal questions.
    b) She will answer a question with a question.
    c) She will ignore the question.
    d) She will say she isn't comfortable discussing the topic.

9. What might be something that is **socially inappropriate** (line 24–25) in your culture?

10. What does **navigating** as it is used in line 32 mean?
    a) Find a balance
    b) Look at a map
    c) Sail a ship
    d) Tell a pilot where to fly

Dialogues/Scenarios

Read the following dialogues and discuss with your classmates.

© RuthChoi/Shutterstock.com

1: A traveler (John) meets a tour guide (Mr. Singh) at the Taj Mahal.

1	John:	Uh, can you help me? I'm looking for the entrance to the Taj Mahal.
2	Mr. Singh:	Sir, you are looking for a tour guide?
3	John:	Well yes. Can you help me?
4	Mr. Singh:	Sir, of course I can. I am from India. I know everything about the Taj Mahal and I have
5		introduced this wonderful treasure to many, many tourists every year.
6	John:	That is very kind of you. How much?
7	Mr. Singh:	I am very cheap. Just 1,000 Rupee.
8	John:	Oh that's not cheap. How about 500 Rupee?
9	Mr. Singh:	Sir, I am the best. I know everything about the Taj and can take you to very special places
10		inside. I will show you, come. 800 Rupee.
11	John:	Okay 800 Rupee. By the way, my name is John (*extends his left hand to Mr. Singh and offers*
12		*to shake on the cost for the guided tour*).
13	Mr. Singh:	Nice to meet you Mr. John Sir. My name is Mr. Singh (*accepts John's hand, but then brushes*
14		*his hand against his pants after the two stop shaking hands*).
15	John:	Likewise Mr. Singh. So where do we go?
16	Mr. Singh:	This way Mr. John Sir, this way. We must hurry because the tour is long and it will get hot
17		soon. Are you ready to see the most incredible sight you have ever seen in all of the world?

Discussion Questions

1. What do John and Mr. Singh do in lines 6 through 11? How is this interaction the same or different in your country? In what places are prices negotiable and where are they fixed?

2. When does John introduce himself? According to John's culture, what do you think is the custom when meeting someone for the first time? What is the custom when meeting someone for the first time in your culture?

3. Why do you think Mr. Singh *brushes his hand against his pants* after they finish shaking hands (lines 13–14)? What social taboo has John possibly violated?

© aphotostory/Shutterstock.com

© Krystof K/Shutterstock.com

2: An American English teacher, Mike, is having dinner with his Taiwanese friend (Yang, Wei) in a night market café.

18	Wei:	Ní hǎo! Hi Mike. How was teaching?
19	Mike:	Ní hǎo. It was good tonight. We talked about American music.
20	Wei:	Oh good. Did you sing for the class?
21	Mike:	No, but they wanted me to. I can't carry a tune so was a little embarrassed. *(Wei's cell phone*
22		*begins to ring.)*
23	Wei:	Wei? Yes, Sara, we're at the night market. We just finished teaching and are going to order
24		some food and drinks. Come join us!
25	Mike:	Wow that's a really cool phone Wei. I like that.
26	Wei:	Here, you can have it.
27	Mike:	Oh, no, no, no. I can't take your phone. I can get one next week after the class pays me.
28	Wei:	No, I insist. Here take it. It's yours. I can get another one. It was very cheap.
29	Mike:	No, Wei. I really don't need a phone. I was just saying I liked it. Now, let's get some dumplings
30		and vegetables.
31	Wei:	Okay, and some beers, but I'm buying.
32	Mike:	Okay, fair enough and yes a beer would be nice.

Discussion Questions

1. What are Wei and Mike doing? What do you think Ní hǎo in Chinese in lines 18 and 19 means?
2. What happens in lines 21–22? Who does Wei begin talking to?
3. How does Wei receive Mike's comment in lines 25–26? What sort of taboo has Mike violated? How do people give and receive compliments in your culture? What might Mike have done differently?

3: Jose, from Mexico, is talking to Thomas, from the United States, about Tom's job as a sales representative for Verizon (a cellphone company).

33	Jose:	So Tom, do you like working for Verizon?
34	Tom:	Ya it's a good company. I get to travel some and I like the people I work for. They're very nice.
35	Jose:	Travel?
36	Tom:	Ya, I went to Miami last week and then next week I'm off to Seattle and then down to Phoenix.
37		So I get to see a lot of the country.
38	Jose:	Nice, so you get paid a lot?
39	Tom:	It's a good salary.
40	Jose	How much do you make?
41	Tom:	Enough to live on. So why are you so interested in Verizon?
42	Jose:	Oh, I saw that they are coming to campus next week and was thinking about giving them my
43		application.
44	Tom:	Well, I can tell you that they really need people who can speak Spanish as well as English. They
45		are really trying to grow their business in places like New Mexico, Arizona, and Texas. Well
46		good luck and let me know if I can help.
47	Jose:	Adios amigo! I gotta get to class.
48	Tom:	Later man.

Discussion Questions

1. What are Jose and Tom talking about? Does Tom like his job? What does he get to do?
2. What taboo does Jose violate in lines 38–40? How does Tom respond to Jose? What might explain Tom's reaction? Is it okay to talk about salaries in your culture? If so, with whom?
3. What does this conversation tell you about Americans?

Activities

Beginning

In the US, it is often said that talking about sex, politics, money, and religion are taboo. Why do you think this is the case? Can you talk about these topics in your country? With whom?

Brainstorm a list of cultural taboos from your first and second cultures. Make a Venn diagram to compare and contrast your first culture with American culture. What is the same and what is different?

Use the following prompts and write sentences about taboo behavior. Use the prompts to compare your first culture with that of another classmate's culture.

In my country, _____ is taboo.

In the US, _____ is/isn't taboo.

Intermediate

Brainstorm a list of cultural taboos with a classmate. Discuss the idea of choices and consequences, and apply it to a discussion about maintaining first-culture taboos in a second-culture environment. Use the following prompts and select a taboo. Write a paragraph (short essay) about positive and negative consequences of following or flouting that behavior in your first and second cultures.

In my first culture, _____ is taboo. If I don't follow it, the consequence may be _____. If that happens, I feel _____. In my second culture, _____ isn't a taboo. If I follow the taboo, the consequence may be _____. If that happens, I feel _____.

Take a field trip to a mall or other public space. Observe the people around you and take notes on their behavior. What is the same or different from your first culture? Do you see behaviors that are taboo to you? What is your reaction to those things? Use your notes to write a short essay about your observations.

Advanced

Create a word web of cultural taboos with your classmates. Discuss similarities and differences between your culture, your classmates' cultures, and American culture. Use the word web as a guide to compare and contrast the social consequences of following or flouting taboos from your first and second cultural perspectives.

Use material from your own life and write about an experience when you encountered a first-culture taboo in a second-culture setting. Use the following questions to guide your writing.

1. What did you see? What was happening?
2. How does this relate to your life?
3. How do you react to that? Is this a problem for you?
4. Why do you think you react in this way?
5. Why do you identify this as a problem or not as a problem?
6. How do you plan to deal with situations like that? (Ilieva, 2001)

Use your personal experiences and work with a partner to create a role-play skit about taboos. Write about your first culture taboos verses American behaviors, or compare your cultural taboos with those of another student. Perform your skit for the class. Afterward, discuss the skit with your classmates. Use the same questions (above) to facilitate your discussion.

Watch a TedTalk or YouTube video that discusses cultural differences or culture clashes. Here's an example of one: https://www.ted.com/watch/ted-institute/ted-state-street/delali-bright-cultural-clashes-in-defining-beauty

Other good online sources to use are *Storycorps:* http://storycorps.org or *This I Believe:* http://thisibelieve.org

Write your reaction to the video. Did you agree or disagree with the speaker or topic? Why? Why not?

Further Reading

Ilieva, R. (2001). Living with ambiguity: Toward culture exploration in adult second-language classrooms. TESL Canada Journal/Revue *TESL du Canada,* 19(1), 1–16.

Chapter 8

Friend Me: Connecting with Friends on Social Networking Sites (SNSs)

Kikuko Omori

© SoleilC/Shutterstock.com

Student Learning Objectives

By the end of this unit, students will be able to:

- ► Understand the cultural differences of forming friendships online.
- ► Identify the appropriate use of social networking sites in the US.

Warm-Up Questions

1. How do you make friends in your country?
2. How do people meet each other in your country?
3. Do you have *Internet* based sites where you can meet people and keep in touch with friends in your country?
4. Do you use a *Social Networking Site* (SNS), like *Facebook* or *LinkedIn*? Do you use language specific SNSs (e.g., *VK, Hyves, Cyworld*) or global SNSs (e.g., *Facebook, LinkedIn*)?
5. Do you know how many *Facebook* friends an average college student has in the US?
6. Do you know how many pictures an average college student posts on *Facebook* in the US?
7. Do you have trouble using SNSs in the US? Why?
8. What do you think the title means? How is the word *friend* being used?

© Bloomua/Shutterstock.com

READING 1

Vocabulary

Stay in touch (vp)	Selfie (n)	Unintended Audience (n)
Profile (n, v)	Vary (v)	Opportunity (n)
Post (n, v)	Value (n)	Present (n, v)
Network (n, v)	Tendency (n)	Tone (n)
Diverse (adj)	Common practice (np)	Nonverbal (adj)
Available (adj)	Boost (v)	Intention (n)
Prevalent (adj)	Self-Esteem (n)	Wisely (adv)
Agents (n)	Lose track of (vp)	Current (adj)

© Angela Waye/Shutterstock.com

Networking and the Internet

1   Social Networking Sites (SNSs) are places on the Internet that were created for people to **stay in touch**
2   with their friends and where they can meet other people online. On SNSs users create their own **profiles**
3   and connect with their friends by sharing **posts** and pictures in the **network**. SNS users can also make
4   comments on others' posts and pictures. For example, on *Facebook* people use "likes" to show their favor
5   on the comments and pictures. Furthermore, SNSs like *Facebook* can repost others' postings by clicking
6   on the "share" button. SNSs became popular communication tools among American college students in
7   the early 2000s. Some researchers found that more than 90% of college students in the US were active
8   SNS users. Since the creation of *SixDegrees.com* in 1997, **diverse** SNSs have become **available** in the US.
9   For example, *Facebook* is especially **prevalent** among college students. One reason for this may be
10   because it was started at Harvard University for Harvard University students. Another popular SNS in
11   the US is *LinkedIn*. It is mostly popular among working professionals. At the same time, regional or lan-
12   guage specific SNSs are popular in different countries such as *VK* (Russia), *Hyves* (The Netherlands),
13   *Cyworld* (South Korea), *Mixi* (Japan), and *RenRen* (China).

© Monkey Business Images/Shutterstock.com

© Andresr/Shutterstock.com

14   Research shows people use the same SNS differently depending on the users' cultural backgrounds.
15   For example, when using Facebook, Indian female users used **agents** such as film stars, dolls, and flowers
16   as their profile pictures while American, Sweden, and Japanese *Facebook* users posted pictures of them-
17   selves and **Selfies** (pictures of oneself taken by oneself) for their profile pictures. In addition, the average
18   number of SNS friends on *Facebook* **varies** across cultures. According to one study, the average numbers
19   of Facebook friends were 513 for American users but only 171 for Japanese users in 2012.

©Rawpixel /Shutterstock.com

20   Having a large social network is **valued** in the US; we can see the **tendency** in online social network-
21   ing sites as well. Furthermore, American college students tend to post a large number of pictures on
22   SNSs. In one study, American college students posted an average of 535 total pictures on *Facebook*. In
23   addition, American Facebook users think of online friends differently than person-to-person friends. In
24   other words, Americans accept friend requests from people they do not know well very easily compared
25   to people from some other countries such as Japan because Americans believe that Facebook friends are
26   just people who communicate online. Having a large number of friends, posting a large number of pic-
27   tures, and using one's own faces as profile pictures are **common practice** for American college students;
28   however, you have the freedom to choose what to post and what not to include in your SNS page. While
29   having a large number of friends, pictures, and using your own face has some advantages, such as, **boost-**
30   **ing** one's own **self-esteem**, creating a unique identity, and easily staying in touch with many friends, there
31   are some risks. For example, by having more than 500 Facebook friends, people tend to **lose track of**
32   names of friends in the network. This could mean your privacy will be **at risk**. Also, you might post pic-
33   tures for fun, but the pictures might be viewed or forwarded to an **unintended audience**. Some people
34   have lost their jobs or lost their **opportunities** to get a job due to inappropriate pictures on SNSs. In addi-
35   tion, international students have to be careful about how to **present** themselves online. Because English
36   may not be their first language, they might not get the **tone** of the postings and run the risk of being
37   misunderstood. Communication using SNSs does not include **nonverbal** cues such as facial expressions
38   and gestures, thus it is hard to judge the writers' **intention** and nuance of the postings. Similarly, even
39   when comments are made as a joke, the comments might be taken differently by other SNS users. More-
40   over, pictures posted on SNSs might be judged totally differently depending on the person who views the
41   pictures. Therefore, it is important to learn how to use SNSs **wisely** when connecting with **current** and
42   old friends all over the world.

Comprehension Questions

1. Define a social networking site (SNS).
2. What are the risks of having a large number of friends on social networking sites?
3. What are the advantages of having a large number of friends on social networking sites?
4. How does culture influence the use of social networking sites?
5. When was the first social networking site created? What is the name of the first social networking site?

6. What is the difference between *Facebook* and *VK*?
7. What is the difference between *Facebook* and *LinkedIn*?
8. What are nonverbal cues?

Vocabulary Activity

1. Using the term "value," please write a paragraph describing the important values in your culture.

2. What does the idiom **"stay in touch"** (line 1) mean?
    a) To remain in physical contact
    b) To be friends
    c) To communicate regularly
    d) To remain behind

3. **Prevalent,** as it is used in line 9, has a similar meaning to which of the following word?
    a) Popular
    b) Relevant
    c) Rare
    d) Important

4. What does **"agents"** mean in line 15?
    a) Spy
    b) Person
    c) Representative
    d) Business

5. Which of the following is a synonym for **"current"** as it is used in line 41?
    a) Present
    b) Time
    c) Flow
    d) Movement

6. Which of the following are common practices for American college students according to the article? (Check all that apply)
    a) Students posting their own faces on Facebook
    b) Uploading a lot of pictures for everyone to see
    c) Liking other peoples' posts
    d) Advertising for a new job on Facebook

7. **"To lose track"** as it is used in line 31 means what?
    a) To fall off the road
    b) To forget about someone or not stay in touch regularly
    c) To not remember someone
    d) To lose your memory

8. Why do people have to be careful about what they post on their SNS?
    a) Their pictures might communicate something different to their online "friends"
    b) Nonverbal cues are not communicated through SNS's
    c) A writer's words may be misinterpreted by the online community
    d) All of the above

9. Can you describe what **"Unintended audience"** means (line 33)? What do you think the prefix "un-" means? Think of other words that begin with prefix "un-".

Discussion Questions

1. Why do you think it's important for American college students to have so many friends on *Facebook*? Is this important to you? Why/Why not?
2. Describe the differences between an online friend and a person-to-person friend. Which would you rather have? Why?
3. According to the reading, SNS's allow people to create a unique identity (line 34). What does this mean? How might a digital identity be different from an offline identity?
4. What are some possible dangers or risks of having a SNS page? Why would the following post be considered dangerous?
   "I'm so excited. I am going to NYC tomorrow for vacation for one week. I can't wait to see the Statue of Liberty and the Empire State Building."
5. What kinds of postings and pictures would be okay in your country and what would not be appropriate?

Activities

Beginning

► The objective of the activity is to create an appropriate profile on *Facebook* within a safe environment. Students will create a profile page that is appropriate for a college student for your class. After creating a profile, students will review others' profile pages and give feedback to each other.

► Alternative: Create a *Facebook* page for the entire class or for your school. (Be sure to get permission from your school administrator before doing this.) What pictures will you use that will capture the "identity" of the class/school?

► Discuss the appropriate topics and pictures you can post on *Facebook* as a college student.

   Which topics are appropriate? Why/Why not?

   1. Post "Happy birthday" on your *Facebook* friend's page.
   2. Post what you have been doing today, which is nothing special, on the wall.
   3. Post the dates when you will be outside of the country on the wall.
   4. Post your cell phone number to your friends on the wall.
   5. Post your political opinions and perspectives on the wall.
   6. Post a cultural event your group is hosting on the wall.

► Learn how to use private settings on *Facebook*. Which contents should you share in public? Which contents do you want to share with a particular group of people?

► Who are you going to send a friend request to? Classmates? A person you just met at the party? Your teachers?

Intermediate

► Explore your classmates' *Facebook* pages. Did you find any discrepancy in their presentation between online and offline? How? Is their online identity the same or different from their offline identity? In what ways?

► Examine celebrities' SNSs and discuss what image they are trying to present online.

► Recently, "*Facebook* addiction" became an issue. Find an article about *Facebook* addiction. Also, after reading the online CNN article (Cohen, 2009) about Facebook addiction: http://www.cnn.com/2009/HEALTH/04/23/ep.facebook.addict/index.html?iref=24hours, summarize the symptoms and issues related to *Facebook* addiction.

Advanced

▶ Discuss in the group about cultural differences of using SNSs after reading the article by Barker and Ota (2011).

▶ Read the article about privacy on *Facebook* in the US (Komando, 2015, http://www.usatoday.com/story/tech/columnist/komando/2015/01/23/facebook-details-sharing/22155437/) and discuss privacy on SNSs.

Further Reading

Barker, V., & Ota H. (2011). Mixi diary versus Facebook photos: Social networking site use among Japanese and Caucasian American females. *Journal of Intercultural Communication Research, 40(1),* 39–63. doi:10.1080/17475759.2011.558321

boyd, d. m., & Ellison, N. B. (2007). Social Network Sites: Definition, history, and scholarship. *Journal of Computer-Mediated Communication, 13,* 210–230. doi:10.1111/j.1083-6101.2007.00393.x.

Cohen, E. (2009, April 23). Five clues that you are addicted to Facebook, *CNN.* Retrieved from http://www.cnn.com/2009/HEALTH/04/23/ep.facebook.addict/index.html?iref=24hours

Komando, K. (2015, January 23). 5 Facebook details you shouldn't share, *USA Today.* Retrieved from http://www.usatoday.com/story/tech/columnist/komando/2015/01/23/facebook-details-sharing/22155437/

Omori, K., & Allen, M. (2014). Cultural differences between American and Japanese self-presentation on SNSs. *The International Journal of Interactive Communication Systems and Technologies, 4* (1), 47–60.

Wrammert, A. (2014). *Selfies, dolls and film stars—a cross-cultural study on how young women in India* (Thesis). Retrieved from: http://www.divaportal.org/smash/get/diva2:721945/FULLTEXT01.pdf

Chapter 9

What Hats Do You Wear?

Michael Schwartz

© PinkPueblo/Shutterstock.com

Student Learning Objectives

By the end of this unit, students will be able to:

- ▶ Describe their different identities.
- ▶ Understand the emotional changes international students experience when they come to the US.
- ▶ Talk about their identity as a learner of English.
- ▶ Understand and use vocabulary associated with identity.
- ▶ Write about their identity.

Warm-Up Questions

1. What kinds of groups or communities do you belong to in your country? These might be family, religious, school, work, or other kinds of groups. Make a list of the different communities you belong to. Are there any that you used to belong to, but now no longer participate in, at least not in the same way?

2. Share this list with your partner. What differences do you see? Do you and your partner belong to similar groups?

3. Are there some groups or communities you belong to where you feel or behave differently? In which groups do you feel most comfortable? Why? In which groups do you feel less comfortable? Why?

4. What do you think the expression "to wear different hats" means?

© iQoncept/Shutterstock.com

Vocabulary

Member (n)	Look to (v)	Depressing (adj)
Behave (v)	Newcomer (n)	Though (adv)
Role (n)	Intimidated (adj)	Adjust (v)
Community (n)	Outsider (n)	Find a balance (vp)
Contribute (v)	Expected (adj)	Accept (v)
Identity (n)	Interaction (n)	Compliment (v)
Gender (n)	Peripheral (adj)	Face-to-face (adj)
Ethnicity (n)	Shape (v)	Doubt (n)
Socioeconomic (n)	Constrained (v)	Confident (adj)
Participate in (vp)	Transition (n)	Reserved (adj)
Create (v)	Traumatic (adj)	

© Anderson74/Shutterstock.com

1   Who am I? This is a question that people often ask themselves. It's a natural part of being a human and
2   of growing up. Our answers to these questions will vary or be different at different times in our lives, even
3   at different times in one day. For example, as a student, we may ask ourselves what we want to learn and
4   do in life when we graduate. At home, though, we may ask ourselves how we can help our family as a son
5   or daughter. What can we do as a **member** in the family to help our mom, dad, or grandparents? We all
6   wear different hats every day. When we are home with our family, we **behave** and talk differently than
7   we do when we are with our friends at school or work. For example, it may be customary for parents to
8   tell their child that they love him or her. But at work, the same person probably does not tell their
9   employees or supervisors that they love them. Rather, they may tell their employees that they are valued
10 and that their hard work for the company is appreciated.
11   These different **roles** and responsibilities we have and the different **communities** we belong to all
12 **contribute** to how we see ourselves and how others see us. This is what is called our **identity**. Some peo-
13 ple think that our identity is fixed, or unchanging, and that our identity can be categorized according to
14 our age, **gender**, **ethnicity**, occupation, marriage, and **socioeconomic** status. They believe that our iden-
15 tity is formed at an early age and that it does not change. Others believe that our identity is constantly
16 changing and evolving on a daily, if not hourly basis. In the example above, the adult's identity is one of
17 parent at home, but at work the same person's identity is one of supervisor or employee. In this way, iden-
18 tity is seen as something that both the individual and the communities they **participate in create**
19 together. What do you think?

© Juergen Priewe/Shutterstock.com

20   In some communities, we may be leaders and the community **looks to** us for leadership, advice, and
21   help. In other communities, we may be members, but we are not seen as leaders. For example, an inter-
22   national student who has been in the United States for a year may be viewed by **newcomers** as a person
23   to ask advice, to help guide newcomers through the process of choosing classes, finding an apartment,
24   and knowing where to eat. However, the same person in a class where he or she is the only international
25   student may feel **intimidated** by his or her "foreign-ness."

© Juergen Priewe/Shutterstock.com

26   He or she may feel like an **outsider** because he or she may not understand the **expected** form of
27   **interaction** in a US classroom between students and teachers and between students and students. Or, the
28   international student may not believe that his or her opinion is valued because he or she comes from a
29   country that is far away and not familiar to the class in general. So the "leader" in the international com-
30   munity may feel like a "visitor" or **peripheral** member in the university class.

© Andrea Danti/Shutterstock.com

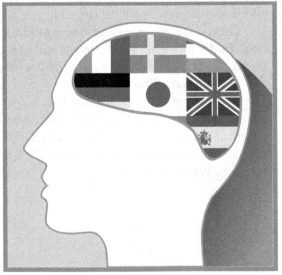

© larm/Shutterstock.com

31   One thing we do know for certain about identity is that the language we speak helps to **shape** our
32   identity because the language we speak is the one we use when we think about ourselves and the one we
33   use with others. Because language influences our identity, researchers have been interested in learning
34   more about how learning another language affects our identity. Some second language learners of
35   English claim they feel and act different when they are speaking English than when they are speaking
36   their home or first language. Others do not believe they feel or act any different. Some people claim that
37   they feel freer or liberated because English offers them the opportunity to be someone different and that

38 they are not controlled by the cultural expectations that exist in their home country. Others, however,
39 feel more **constrained** or confined because English has too many grammar and writing rules or because
40 they are unable to feel the deep emotions associated with words like *love* or *hate* and so prefer to use their
41 own language to express their feelings. Still others believe they have lost a part of their identity due to
42 learning English because English was imposed on them as a school subject when they were in middle
43 and high school.

44   For international students, coming to the United States to study English and/or to earn a college
45 degree, the **transition** from their home country to the United States can be very difficult or **traumatic**.
46 Many will encounter culture shock and even language shock. Culture shock is cyclical, with the first few
47 days or weeks being one of great joy and discovery. Everything is new and different and this can be very
48 exciting. After a while though, students will begin to miss their home, their families and friends, their
49 food, their music, and more. Suddenly their new surroundings are no longer fun and exciting, but are
50 **depressing** and aggravating. When this happens, students often get angry very quickly and begin to hate
51 everything about the new culture and wish they were back home instead. Over time **though**, students
52 begin to **adjust** and **find a balance**. They form a new circle of friends and become involved in activities
53 outside of school. They also learn to **accept** that some things are just different in the US and that this is
54 neither good nor bad, but just different.

© Qoncept/Shutterstock.com

55   Language shock is related to culture shock. It, too, can cause depression. Language shock is what
56 some students experience when they think their English language skills are better than they are. In their
57 home country, where they began learning English, they performed very well, receiving good grades in
58 their classes and being **complimented** by their teachers, family, and friends. They may even have scored
59 very well on a national or international English test like TOEFL® or IELTS. When they arrive in the
60 United States, though, they experience a different kind of English, or "real English" as opposed to "book
61 English." At a university, they even come **face-to-face** with "academic English," which is very formal Eng-
62 lish and is quite different from social or conversational English.

63   Both culture shock and language shock influence a person's identity. At first they can create **doubt**
64 in a person. Someone who was once highly **confident** in his or her first language and culture is suddenly
65 unsure of him or herself. A person who is experiencing language and culture shock may become quiet
66 and more **reserved**, and choose not to participate in activities that he or she once did. This is because the
67 familiar communities and knowing the social rules of behavior have all changed.

68   Whether you have experienced culture shock or language shock, coming to the United States has had
69 some influence on you and your identity. The question is in what ways and how has your identity
70 changed? Are these changes for the better or the worse?

Discussion Questions

1. What is culture shock? Have you experienced culture shock and how did you cope with it?
2. What is language shock? Did you experience language shock when you arrived in the United States? How did you handle the differences you encountered?
3. Do you think a person's identity changes? If so, how and what causes these changes? If not, why not?
4. How much influence do other communities have on your identity? How much influence does your home language have on you and how much influence does English have on your identity?
5. Look back at your list of communities. Can you describe how you act in each of these communities? What language and what kind of language (informal, formal, other) do you use in these communities?

Comprehension/Vocabulary

1. What is the main idea of this article?
   a) People like to wear different kinds of hats at work to express their identity.
   b) Our identity does not change.
   c) Our identity is influenced by us and by the people around us.
   d) We have different identities at home and at school.

2. List the categories that are common identity descriptors.
   a)
   b)
   c)
   d)
   e)
   f)

3. Why might an international student feel intimidated in a university class?
   a) He or she doesn't understand the language.
   b) He or she doesn't understand the culture of the US classroom.
   c) He or she has bad opinions about the topic of discussion.
   d) He or she is busy helping newcomers adjust to the US.

4. Can you think of other reasons why an international student might feel intimidated in a US classroom?

5. What does "shape" mean in line 31?
   a) Cut
   b) Form
   c) Draw
   d) Take

6. Why might some people feel like they have lost their identity because of English?
   a) Because there are too many rules.
   b) Because it is too formal.
   c) Because they cannot feel love or hate.
   d) Because they were forced to learn it at school.

7. What are some of the causes of "Language Shock"? Can you think of others?
    a)
    b)
    c)
    d)

8. Which of the following is not a possible synonym for **"reserved"** as it is used in line 66?
    a) Outgoing
    b) Withdrawn
    c) Private
    d) Reticent

Speak English
By Hasmukh Amathala

(from http://www.poemhunter.com)

I speak English
But do not wish
Goodness in foreign language
My own language is good to manage

National language is good link
We must always think
In terms of good communication
Hand signs are best indication

No doubt English is powerful medium
But its use is bare minimum
Only handful people speak and understand
Rest all speak only name sake as current trend

Sometimes it is lack of knowledge
Sometimes it is not grasping good page
Language is after all language
Rich or poor but helps in crucial phase

Go to out side country
Our language may not be understood by many
So the English comes in picture
To bring smile on face for sure

Submitted: Friday, April 18, 2014
Edited: Friday, April 18, 2014
Reprinted with permission by the author.

1. In the poem *Speak English*, what is Hasmukh trying to balance?
2. What does Hasmukh mean in the third stanza, "No doubt English is powerful medium but its use is bare minimum."
3. At the beginning of the poem Hasmukh does not like English, "I speak English but do not wish." How do his feelings about English change by the end of the poem? Why?

4. Does this poem reflect your feelings about English? Why or why not?
5. Does this poem reflect your identity as a learner of English? How? If not, what is your identity as a learner of English?

Activities

Beginning

▶ Make two flags or two posters. Make one flag/poster that represents your identity as a native speaker of your home language and your home country. Make the other flag/poster showing your identity as a learner of English and as a student in the United States. How are they the same? How are they different?

▶ Using the poem above, or another poem, make a video or song expressing the feelings you have about learning English.

▶ Make your own avatars using http://bitstrips.com/create/avatar/ Create one that represents your home identity and one that represents your identity as a learner of English. What's the same? What's different? Why?

▶ Write your own "Biopoem" (Abromitis, 1994). Do a Google search for how to write a biopoem. This document is also available online at: http://spencerlibrary.com/services/biopoem.pdf

Intermediate

▶ Go to http://www.poemhunter.com and find more poems about learning English. Choose one to discuss with the class. Why did you choose this particular poem? Describe how it reflects or does not reflect your feelings about English.

▶ Write a poem or song about your identity as a learner of English. Post it on http://www.poemhunter.com or another website.

▶ Write a short story about an experience that you have had recently. How has this experience influenced your identity?

▶ Keep a journal of your experiences and emotions for a week or a month. After the week or month is finished, re-read your entries. What, if any changes, have you experienced? Did you feel your identity was threatened or undervalued in some situations? Where did you feel your identity was valued and respected? Describe these contexts in a short paper, poem, song, video, or combination of various media.

▶ Do an Internet search to find out more about "Culture Shock" and "Language Shock." What are the causes for these phenomena? What are their symptoms? How can you help someone who is struggling with Culture Shock and/or Language Shock? Reflect on your own experiences with Culture Shock and/or Language Shock?

Advanced

▶ Listen to the following segment from NPR "Author Explores Irony and Identity in a 'A Chinaman's Chance'"

http://www.npr.org/blogs/codeswitch/2014/08/12/339541058/author-explores-irony-and-identity-in-a-chinamans-chance

Take notes on the segment and be prepared to talk about the segment in class. What has your identity journey with English been?

► Find copies of Amy Tan's "Mother Tongue." Read and discuss with the class. Have students write their own essays on their experiences with using their home language and English. Where do they use their home language and where do they use English? How do they feel when they use English? Is there an additive effect to their identity or a subtractive effect?

► Create a survey about identity and distribute it to other international students or even to both international students and domestic students. Tabulate the results and give a presentation on your findings.

► Get copies of the article *The classroom and the wider culture: Identity as a key to learning English Composition* by Fan Shen (1989). Discuss with your class and write about your own experiences learning English and the influences this experience has had on your identity.

Further Reading

Abromitis, B. S. (1994, June/July). Bringing lives to life. Biographies in reading and the content areas. *Reading today 11*(6), p. 26.

Block, D. (2009). *Second language identities.* London: Continuum International Publishing Group.

Hoffman, E. (1989). *Lost in translation: A life in a new language.* New York: Penguin Books.

Chapter 10

Under the Gun: The Culture of Firearms and Hunting in the USA

Alexandra Yarbrough

A WELL REGULATED MILITIA BEING NECESSARY TO THE SECURITY OF A FREE STATE, THE RIGHT OF THE PEOPLE TO KEEP AND BEAR ARMS SHALL NOT BE INFRINGED

© igitalreflections/Shutterstock.com

Student Learning Objectives

By the end of this unit, students will be able to:

- ► Understand the history of guns and gun ownership in the USA.
- ► Describe their opinions on the subject of guns and gun ownership.
- ► Understand and use the vocabulary associated with guns and gun ownership.
- ► Write about guns and gun ownership.
- ► Learn about hunting in the United States.
- ► Talk about why hunting is a popular hobby in the USA.
- ► Discuss the relationship between hunting and gun ownership.
- ► Use English idioms associated with guns and hunting.

Warm-Up Questions

1. Think about guns in your country. Who is allowed to own a gun? Where can people buy guns? Are there any special rules about who can own a gun and when they can have it?
2. Share these facts with a partner from another country. What differences do you see? Are there any similarities? If there is no one from another country, share these ideas with someone from your country. Do any of them surprise you? Did your partner and you have the same facts?
3. What do you think the expression "the right to bear arms" means?
4. How do you feel about the current laws of gun ownership in your country? Do you agree with all of them? Do you wish things would change? Why?
5. Look up the idiom *under the gun* and discuss what it means. Do you have a similar expression in your language?

© Stephanie Frey/Shutterstock.com

READING 1

Vocabulary

Revolution (n)	Right (n)	Assault (v)
Legislation (n)	Arrest (v)	Prohibit (v)
Benefit (v)	Controversial (adj)	Criminal (n)
Protest (v)	Amendment (n)	Incidence (n)
Deny (v)	Regulate (v)	Debate (v)
Define (v)	Militia (n)	Interpretation (n)
Individual (adj)	Infringe (v)	Affect (v)
Founding Fathers (n)	Essentially (adv)	Convicted felon(n)
Constitution (n)	Weapons (n)	Privilege (n)
Create (v)	Defense (n)	

The Right to Bear Arms

1   Before the American **Revolution** in 1776, colonists were forced to follow all British rules and **legislation**.
2   Many colonists disagreed with these rules because the rules were made to **benefit** the British, not the
3   colonists. American colonists began to disagree and **protest** these rules. When American colonists began
4   to complain about the British rules, England started to **deny** or take away many of the colonists' rights.

© igorlale/Shutterstock.com

5   Following the American Revolutionary War, American leaders wanted to **define** what the **individu-**
6   **al's** rights were. Colonists wanted to be certain that no one could ever take away their freedoms again.
7   The **Founding Fathers** wrote the **Constitution** so that all American citizens would know what their
8   rights were and understand that no one had the power to take these freedoms away.
9   The Founding Fathers **created** the Bill of Rights[1] in 1791 (10 fundamental **rights** for American citi-
10 zens). The Bill of Rights says things like the government can't stop Americans from practicing their reli-
11 gion, that Americans can practice whatever religion they want, that if an American is **arrested** they have
12 a right to a fast trial, and that the government can't keep an American in jail without giving them a trial.
13 One of the most **controversial amendments** is the <u>second amendment</u>. The second amendment
14 says, "A well **regulated militia**, being necessary to the security of a free State, the right of the people to

---

1. http://billofrightsinstitute.org/founding-documents/bill-of-rights/

keep and bear Arms, shall not be **infringed**."[2] This **essentially** means that the government can't stop Americans from having and carrying **weapons** because Americans may need them for **defense**. This may seem like a strange right to include in the top 10 list of rights. However, the colonists had just fought a war to protect themselves from an unfair government. These leaders believed that people had the right to protect themselves against **assault** even if the attack came from a government. Americans wanted the right to have weapons for their future protection.

However for the last eighty years, the US government has written several gun control laws. Some of these laws are controversial because people believe the second amendment protects their right to have and carry guns. The government believes that people should have the right to have weapons. However, the government also believes there should be checks and controls on this right. Some of these checks include things like **prohibiting criminals** and the mentally ill from owning guns, imposing a tax on machine guns, and recording the sale of guns. Most of these new laws have been introduced after an **incidence** of gun violence[3].

© bikeriderlondon/Shutterstock.com

The right to own and carry guns is now hotly **debated** in the United States. There are several different **interpretations** of the second amendment[4]. These different **interpretations affect** gun ownership in the US. The second amendment gives a "well regulated militia" the right to own and carry guns. People now **debate** who this "militia" really is.

On one side, there are people who say that the "militia" refers to an armed citizen. They believe that individuals have the right to own and carry guns and that this is a fundamental right of being a citizen of the United States and there shouldn't be any restrictions. (However they do acknowledge that there are certain people who shouldn't own guns: the mentally insane or **convicted** felons.)

On the other side, there are people who say that the "well regulated militia" is actually a government-led group. According to them, individual citizens do not have the right to own guns because it is a **privilege** given by the government. There are of course people who stand somewhere in the middle of the debate. As long as there is gun violence in the United States, people will continue to debate a person's right to own and carry guns.

Currently, there are an estimated 270,000,000 to 310,000,000 guns in the USA[5]. This amounts to about 102 guns for every 100 people. The USA is ranked No. 1 internationally in the number of privately owned guns[6]. The USA is also classified as a "major" manufacturer of small, medium, and major firearms[7].

2. http://www.npr.org/templates/story/story.php?storyId=91942478
3. http://www.npr.org/templates/story/story.php?storyId=91942478
4. http://www.theatlantic.com/magazine/archive/2011/09/the-secret-history-of-guns/308608/
5. http://www.gunpolicy.org/firearms/region/united-states
6. http://www.gunpolicy.org/firearms/region/united-states
7. http://www.gunpolicy.org/firearms/region/united-states

Discussion Questions

1. Why is the Bill of Rights important to Americans? Do you have a document in your country that outlines the rights and freedoms of citizens?
2. What is the most important right you have in your country? Why?
3. Is this a topic that is debated in your country?
4. Do you own a gun? Do you know anyone who owns a gun? How would you feel if you went to a friend's house for dinner and there were guns there?
5. Do you think that owning a gun should be a right? Or is it a privilege?
6. What do you think is the impact of gun control laws? Should there be regulations about who can own a gun? What kind of regulations?

Comprehension/Vocabulary

1. The main idea of this text is:
    a) Many people in the USA have guns.
    b) Guns are essentially a dangerous part of American culture and Americans are now trying to stop individual ownership.
    c) Owning guns is a fundamental right and every person in the USA should have the right to protect themselves.
    d) The right to own guns comes from the Bill of Rights and is still a debated topic in the USA.

2. What might be another word used for **created** in line 9.
    a) Wrote
    b) Imported
    c) Thought
    d) Believed

3. What are the two main opinions about the right to own guns in the USA?
    a)
    b)

4. Why did the colonists originally want the right to own guns?

5. Legislators made restrictions about who could own guns. Who are two groups that think people should *not* own guns?
    a)
    b)

6. Which of the following words would best complete the sentence below:

    The thief who robbed a convenience store last week has been _____ and taken to the local jail.

    a) assaulted
    b) defined
    c) arrested
    d) created

7. Which of the following is a synonym for **infringed** as it is used in line 15?
   a) Taken away
   b) Allowed
   c) Put up with
   d) Bothered

8. Which of the following is <u>NOT</u> a **weapon** (line 17)?
   a) Gun
   b) Knife
   c) Sword
   d) Militia

9. What does **amendment** mean as it is used in line 13?
   a) Change, modification, or adjustment in some way.
   b) Deletion, cancelation, or elimination in some way.
   c) Revolution, conviction, or resistance to something.
   d) Creation, invention, or discovery of something.

10. Describe the difference between **right** (lines 9–11) and **privilege** (lines 49–50)?

11. If a person is **convicted** (line 47) of a crime, the person is . . .
    a) Set free
    b) Brought to trial
    c) Given a gun
    d) Found guilty

READING 2

©MIGUEL GARCIA SAAVEDRA/Shutterstock.com

© Bruce MacQueen/Shutterstock.com

© Steve Oehlenschlager/Shutterstock.com

Pre-Reading Questions

1. Is hunting legal in your country? Why or why not?
2. If hunting is legal in your country, what sorts of animals and/or birds do people hunt?
3. Why do you think some people like to hunt?
4. What do you think about hunting? Is hunting a good thing or bad? Why?
5. Are there any animals or birds that you think should not be hunted? Why?
6. What do you think the idiom "happy hunting" means?

Vocabulary

Shotgun (n)	Interior (n)	Heirloom (n)
Pistol (n)	Civilization (n)	Accuracy (n)
Rifle (n)	Necessity (n)	Bullet (n)
Bow & Arrow (n)	Hobby (n)	BBs (n)
Season (n)	Permission (n)	Target (n)
Game (n)	Bag (v)	Pattern (n)
Shoot (v)	Lure in (vp)	Permission (n)
Provide (v)	Time-honored tradition (np)	Trespassing (n)
Love affair (np)	Passed down (vp)	Hunting reserve (np)

Hunting: Happy Hunting

1 In the first reading, "The Right to Bear Arms" you learned
2 that Americans are guaranteed the right to own a gun for
3 self-protection and that the historical reason for this is
4 because Americans during the 1770s were afraid of the
5 British soldiers. While this is true, there is another reason
6 why Americans have a **love affair** with guns: hunting. In
7 fact, hunting was a necessity for the early colonists and
8 later for the pioneers who began traveling west into the
9 **interior** of what is now the United States. Like other **civi-**
10 **lizations**, before there were convenient grocery stores to
11 buy meat, fruits, and vegetables, people had to produce
12 their own source of food. The pioneers of the 1800s in the
13 US left the big cities, like New York, Philadelphia, and Bos-
14 ton and moved west to places that we now call Ohio, Ken-
15 tucky, or Missouri. Moving west meant the pioneers had to
16 find other sources of food, such as growing their own veg-
17 etables and hunting wild animals.
18   Today, hunting is not a necessity for most Americans
19 as it was in the 1800s for the pioneers. Today, it is more of
20 a hobby. Many people, men, women, and children, enjoy
21 the fall or autumn because it means **hunting season's** open

© Steve Oehlenschlager/Shutterstock.com

22 for many different kinds of **game**. People can hunt such animals and birds as deer, rabbits, squirrels,
23 ducks, geese, dove, and pheasants. People will go out into the woods or on to open farmlands where they
24 have **permission** to hunt and try to **bag** a deer or pheasant. Or they will go to a lake or small body of
25 water and try to **lure in** ducks and geese and then shoot them. Hunting is a **time-honored tradition** in
26 the United States and a **hobby** that is **passed down** from generation to generation. In addition to the
27 hobby itself, many families own guns that have been in the family for a hundred years or more. They are
28 considered to be valuable family **heirlooms** and are not to be sold or given to strangers or non-family
29 members.

© Zorandim/Shutterstock.com

© Canon Boy/Shutterstock.com

© Marcel Jancovic/Shutterstock.com

30 The guns and other weapons used for hunting include **shotguns**, **rifles**, and **bow & arrows**. While
31 some hunters do carry **pistols**, these are not typically used for hunting because a bullet fired from a pis-
32 tol loses its **accuracy** over a very short distance. Rifles, however, can be accurate for up to 100–150 yards
33 or more depending on the rifle. Rifles tend to be used for hunting big game, like deer, elk, antelope, and
34 even bear. Shotguns are better suited for small game, like rabbits and squirrels as well as birds, such as
35 geese, ducks, dove, and pheasants. This is because a shotgun shoots several hundred pellets, or **BBs**, at
36 one time. This allows the hunter to shoot a small and fast moving target because the BB **pattern** covers
37 a wide diameter, usually around 30 inches. Because of the large **target** area of shotguns, they are some-
38 times called "scatter guns." A rifle, on the other hand, only shoots one **bullet** at a time. Thus it would be
39 extremely difficult to shoot and hit a small, fast-moving animal with a rifle. Shooting and hitting a large
40 animal, from a greater distance is more suited for a rifle.
41 Some people like to hunt with a bow and arrow too. Animals that are hunted with a bow and arrow
42 are typically deer and turkey. There are special seasons and licenses for hunting with a bow and arrow.
43 One of the exciting things about hunting with a bow and arrow is that the hunter has to get very close to
44 the deer or turkey, meaning that the hunter gets to see up close the wild game, much like seeing wild
45 animals in a zoo up close, only the animals are not behind a glass wall or cage like they are in a zoo.

© Suzi Nelson/Shutterstock.com

46   Hunting is a wonderful sport and is enjoyed by many people in every state. However, hunting can
47   also be dangerous and there are many rules that people must follow. For example, people cannot hunt
48   ducks all year long. They can only hunt ducks in the fall and early winter during "duck season," and they
49   can only shoot so many ducks in a day. Also, hunters must have a license to hunt and most states today
50   require that hunters take a hunter safety course before being given a license. Finally, hunters must get
51   **permission** from farmers to go on to their land to hunt. If they don't, this is called **trespassing** and is a
52   serious crime. Hunters can also go to **hunting reserves** but these are often very expensive and some even
53   require a club membership to join.
54   When it comes to the debates about gun ownership and gun control as described in the first reading,
55   guns made for hunting, shotguns and hunting rifles, are not usually what people want to control or make
56   illegal. It is guns that can be easily hidden, like a pistol, and guns made for war, like assault rifles. Because
56   hunting is part of American history and because it is important to so many family histories, it will con-
58   tinue to be part of American culture and will play a significant role in the debates over gun ownership
59   and control for years to come.

Comprehension and Vocabulary Questions

1. According to the reading, why do Americans like hunting?
    a) Family tradition
    b) They have to for food
    c) There are no grocery stores in America
    d) It reminds Americans of fall or autumn

2. Which of the following animals are not hunted according to the article.
    a) Rabbits
    b) Deer
    c) Eagles
    d) Ducks

3. What does **"passed down"** mean as it is used in line 26?
    a) To die
    b) To give to a younger family member
    c) To throw away
    d) To go by something

4. A gun that has been owned by the same family for several generations might be called what?
    a) A shotgun
    b) A rifle
    c) A pistol
    d) An heirloom

5. Write the word for the appropriate weapon for the following Game Animal or Bird.
    a) Deer
    b) Goose
    c) Turkey
    d) Bear
    e) Rabbit
    f) Pheasant
    g) Squirrel
    h) Duck

6. Which of the following might represent a shotgun pattern and a bullet pattern?

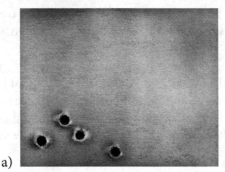
a)

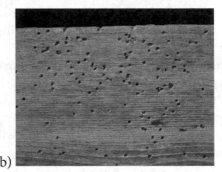
b)

© Andrey_Kuzmin/Shutterstock.com   ©Chris H. Galbraith/Shutterstock.com

7. Which of the following must a hunter do before going out to hunt?
    a) Get a license to hunt
    b) Get permission to hunt on privately owned farmland
    c) Take a hunter safety course
    d) All of the above

8. How does the sport of hunting complicate the issue of gun ownership and gun control in the United States? Discuss with your partners and with the class.

Activities

Beginning

▶   Make a poster that compares the gun laws and norms to your country and that of the US. What is the same? What is different? What do you like about the United States' rules? What do you like about your country's rules?

Intermediate

Local News

Chai Soua Vang was born in Laos in 1968. Vang and his father fought with the anti-communist movement (The USA) during the Vietnam War. However, when the United States began to pull troops out of Vietnam, Vang's family was forced to move to the United States. They moved to Sacramento, California, in 1980 and later moved to Minneapolis, Minnesota, in 2000. Vang had six children, was the family Shaman, and was an avid hunter.

One weekend, Vang and his friend went deer hunting in Wisconsin. Vang was thought to be in an area of the land that he shouldn't have been in. Another hunter told Vang to leave and Vang walked to another trail. However, several more hunters followed Vang on ATVs (small vehicles) to confront Vang about his trespassing. No one really knows what happened that day. But Vang is believed to have shot eight people. Six of them are now dead.

There is some debate now about racism, the right to hunt, the effects of Post-Traumatic Stress Disorder, the right to own guns, and gun safety and how all of these factors may have influenced this day.

Vang was later shot and killed.

The following is a link to the poem "If in America" by Ed Bok Lee. It was written in reaction to the shooting in Wisconsin. Read this with your class and discuss it. How does it make you feel?

http://www.poetryfoundation.org/poem/247390

Idiom Practice

Here are two lists of idioms. One is for guns in general and one is for hunting. Can you figure out what they mean? Ask a fluent speaker of English what they mean and then make a chart or poster that shows their meaning. The chart or poster can be pictures, definitions, or something else.

Guns

1. Big gun
2. Smoking gun
3. Great guns
4. Gun it
5. Jump the gun
6. Hired gun
7. Stick to one's guns
8. Under the gun
9. Going great guns
10. Gun down
11. Give it your best shot

Hunting

1. Hunt something or someone down
2. Hunt for something
3. Hunt down
4. Head hunter
5. That dog won't hunt

6. Fair game
7. Bark up the wrong tree
8. Call off the dogs
9. Hound someone
10. A sitting duck
11. Open season
12. Lower your sights

Advanced

▶ Create a survey to ask other people about their opinions on the "right to bear arms." Interview other people on campus and compare results with classmates.

▶ Split the class into two groups. Each group will research an organization in the United States: The NRA and The Brady Campaign. What do the two groups want? Why are they so different? What are their motivations? Who currently holds more power? Why and how do they hold more power? Who do you agree with? Do you have any equivalent groups in your country?

▶ Debate: Split the class into groups to debate the right to bear arms. Allow the groups time to research and prepare for the debate beforehand. Assign judges to decide who scored more points and on what merit.

▶ Watch a Hunter Safety video on YouTube like the following video. Discuss what you see and learn with your class. https://www.youtube.com/watch?v=U6FXxgLKupo

▶ Research the Sandy Hook Elementary, Virginia Tech, or Charleston, South Carolina shooting. Or watch a video about them (Virginia Tech: https://www.youtube.com/watch?v=UpZ0F1rGBjc Sandy Hook: https://www.youtube.com/watch?v=6X7cVDxYd6A) Discuss whether you think these shootings could have been prevented or how they shaped the discussion about gun control in the USA. Did either of these videos change your views on gun control? Has there ever been a shooting in your country similar to the circumstances to these school shootings?

Chapter 11

Don't Throw the Baby Out with the Bath Water

Michael Schwartz

© Michelle D. Milliman/Shutterstock.com

© Giulio_Fornasar/Shutterstock.com

© Robert Kneschke/Shutterstock.com

Student Learning Objectives

By the end of this unit, students will be able to:

▶ Discuss bathing, grooming, and hygienic habits around the world.

▶ Use essential vocabulary related to hygiene.

▶ Talk with a barber or hair stylist.

▶ Understand different attitudes and beliefs about beauty products.

Discussion Questions

Read the questions below and write your answers on a piece of paper. Then share your answers with your group.

1. How often do people bathe in your country? Is this different for adults and children?
2. When, or at what time of the day, do people bathe in your country? Are there special occasions when someone would or would not bathe in your country?
3. How do people feel about facial hair in your country?
4. Are their special hairstyles that men or women have in your country?
5. Who uses make-up or cosmetics in your country?
6. What do you think the title of this chapter means and where you do think the expression comes from?

© Janis Smits/Shutterstock.com

READING 1

Vocabulary

Shampoo (n, v)	Hygiene (n)	Offensive (adj)
Conditioner (n)	Shower (n, v)	Attractive (adj)
Deodorant (n)	Bath (n)	Rinse off (vp)
Bathtub (n)	Bathe (v)	Take a shower (vp)
Perfume (n)	Scrub (v)	
Body Odor (n)	Soap down (vp)	

Bathing Habits

1   Around the world, cultures have different **hygiene** habits. Some cultures bathe once a week. Others will
2 **take a shower** every day. For some cultures, showering is a nightly routine before going to bed. For oth-
3 ers, it is a morning activity to help them get ready for the day. Some cultures put on sweet smelling
4 deodorants or perfumes while others prefer the natural scent of body odor. In some countries, the bath-
5 room and the shower are all one large room with the shower being located very close to the toilet. In
6 other cultures, the shower and bathtub are separate parts of the bathroom, while in other cultures the
7 room where the toilet is located in a completely different room from where people shower or bathe.

© Glaze Image/Shutterstock.com   © LukaTDB/Shutterstock.com

8   Many Americans are shower-happy. They like to **shower** frequently. Some people will take a shower
9 two or three times a day; once when they get up, once after they finish exercising or working out, and
10 then again at night before going to bed. Other people prefer to take a bath, meaning they like to sit in the
11 **bathtub** and soak in hot water, sometimes with lots of soapy bubbles, for a long time. People that like to
12 **bathe** often take a book or magazine with them so they can read while bathing. It seems like Americans
13 are obsessed with bathing, either in the shower or in a bathtub. Why? It wasn't always this way.

© Hein Nouwens/Shutterstock.com

14   Before indoor plumbing, water for drinking, cooking, and bathing had to be carried in from a well
15 or large water trough that was outside the house. Then it had to be heated on a wood stove before it could
16 be used for bathing. To take a bath, the person would get into a large tub, sit down, and pour hot water
17 into the tub. Then the person would **soap down**, **scrub**, and then more hot water was added to help the
18 person **rinse off**.

19   When Americans were leaving the big cities like New York, Philadelphia, and Baltimore and moving
20 out west to live on the plains of Missouri, Kansas, or Texas during the 1800s, bathing was even more of
21 a chore and people might go weeks or months between baths. Water oftentimes had to be carried from a
22 lake or river that was several miles from the house. For this reason, the settlers or pioneers used the same
23 bath water for the whole family so they could conserve their water supply for drinking, cooking, and
24 cleaning. As the story goes, the father would bathe first, then the mother, then the oldest child, then the
25 next, and so on until the last person to get a bath was the baby. By the time the baby was put in the bath-
26 tub, the water was black from all of the dirt that had washed off the other bathers.. It would have been
27 easy to lose a baby in the dirty bath water. This is where the expression, "**Don't throw the baby out with**
28 **the bathwater**" comes from. Today the expression has a very different meaning: to not give up because
29 of one problem.

30   Today, with indoor plumbing, it is now possible to bathe every day. Some people even shower two or
31 three times a day. Most Americans take a shower in the morning when they first wake up. Others will
32 shower at the end of the day before going to bed. Still others will shower both in the morning and in the
33 evening. For those who work out, they might shower after exercising too. Why do Americans bathe so
34 much? The most basic answer is that they don't want to smell. They don't like to stink and they think
35 **body odor** is offensive. Rather, Americans like to smell like flowers or fresh rain or a forest. To smell
36 sweet, Americans put on **deodorant** and **perfumes** and wash their hair and bodies with scented **sham-**
37 **poos**, **conditioners**, and soap. Finally, after they step out of the shower, they put on deodorant and per-
38 fumes so they smell sweet all day long and to hide body odor.

Comprehension Questions

1. What is the main idea of Reading 1?
   a) How to take a shower
   b) American bathing habits
   c) Where the expression, "Don't throw the baby out with the bathwater" comes from
   d) Ways in which Americans hide body odor

2. Why do Americans shower or bathe so frequently?
   a) Because they think body odor is offensive
   b) Because they like indoor plumbing
   c) Because they exercise everyday
   d) Because they like to smell like flowers

3. Why did the early American settlers and pioneers use the same bathwater for the whole family?
   a) They thought it was healthy
   b) They didn't like taking baths
   c) They moved out of big cities like New York and Philadelphia
   d) They needed to conserve water for multiple purposes

4. Do you think it's healthy to bathe or shower every day? Why? Or Why not?

Vocabulary

Choose the best word or phrase from the list below to complete the sentences. Note there are more words in the table than there are blanks.

shampooing	fragrances	conditioner
deodorant	rinse off	shower
body odor	hygiene	
bathe	scrub	

1. After someone has finished _____ their hair, they will sometimes use _____ to rinse the soap out and to leave their hair soft and easy to brush or comb.

2. In some cultures _____ is not considered offensive and people do not worry about how they might smell.

3. _____ are usually sweet smelling scents like flowers or fresh rain.

4. Everyone, everywhere wants to be clean, but _____ habits and what it means to be clean is different from culture to culture.

5. My mother used to say "remember to _____ behind your ears" because this is a place where dirt can hide and be difficult to remove.

6. To relieve stress, some people like to _____ by soaking in a bathtub of hot water. Others like to stand in the _____ having hot water run over them for a long time.

© fiphoto/Shutterstock.com

© Kostsov/Shutterstock.com

© Tyler Olson/Shutterstock.com

READING 2

Vocabulary

get _____ hair done (vp)	bangs (n)	hairstylist (n)
trim (n)	moustache (n)	barber (n)
take a little off the _____ (vp)	beard (n)	beautician (n)
sideburns (n)	hairstyle (n)	

Warm-Up Questions

1. Where do people go to get haircuts in your countries?
2. How often or frequently do people get their hair done in your countries?
3. What's the difference between the two statements below?
   a) You cut your hair.
   b) You got your hair cut.
4. How do people feel about facial hair (beards, moustaches, and side-burns) in your country?
5. How do people feel about long hair, especially on men, in your country?
6. What do people talk about when they get a haircut in your country?
7. What might be typical conversation topics while getting your haircut in the US?
8. What do all of the pictures above have in common?
9. What do hair salons or barbershops look like in your country?

Time for a Trim

1   Terri: Hi, are you Jonathan?
2   Jon: Yep, that's me.
3   Terri: Well come on back and let's **get your hair done**.
4   Jon: Thanks. It's been a while since I've had a haircut.
5   Terri: So what are we doing today?
6   Jon: Oh, I guess I'd like you to **trim** the bangs, **take a little off the top** and sides, and even out the
7   **sideburns**.
8   Terri: Okay, what about the back?
9   Jon: Oh, ya, just trim it a touch. Don't forget to get the bangs. When they get long, it gets difficult to
10   see, you know.
11 Terri: Would you like me to touch up your **moustache** and **beard** too?
12 Jon: No, I can do that at home, but thanks.
13 Terri: So what else are you doing today?
14 Jon: Ah, after this I'm heading to the store to pick up some groceries and then I thought I'd watch a
15   movie tonight. And you, what are you doing?
16 Terri: After work, my husband and children and I are going to see the baseball game.
17 Jon: You like baseball? Who's your favorite team?
18 Terri: The Twins of course, but they're not doing real well this year. I was thinking they might have a
19   better team this year with a new manager, but it looks like it's going to take more than that.
20 Jon: Yep, I agree. I'm a Yankee's fan, but they're not playing well this year either.
21 Terri: Well there you go. How does it look?

22	Jon:	Oh this is great. This feels much better. Thanks!
23	Terri:	You're welcome. That'll be $13.00.
24	Jon:	Here's the 13 and another $2.00 for you. Enjoy the game.
25	Terri:	Thanks Jon, will do. See you in about 3 weeks.

Discussion Questions

1. How does the beginning sequence (lines 1–11) between Terri and Jon begin? What's the purpose of this sequence?
2. What does Jon ask Terri to do with his hair? What do you think "take a little off the top" means?
3. In lines 12–21, Terri and Jon change the topic of their conversation. Why? What kinds of things do people talk about when getting their hair done in your countries?
4. What time of year do you think it is?
5. In the last sequence, what does Jon do? Why does he give Terri $15.00 instead of $13.00? Is this common in your countries?
6. What is the difference between a barber, a beautician, and a hairstylist? Who is Jon getting his haircut from today? Why do you think this?

Vocabulary

Choose the best word or phrase from the list below to complete the sentences. Note there are more words in the table than there are blanks. There may be multiple answers for some blanks.

bangs	barber	hairstylist
trim	get my hair done	moustache
beautician	sideburns	
take a little off the top	hairstyle	

1. Okay, so the wedding is at 2:00 p.m. That means I need to make an appointment with my _____ for 10:00 a.m.

2. I've been wearing my hair the same way for 5 years. I'm tired of it. I need to get a new _____. The next time I _____ I'm going to talk to my _____ and ask her if she can do something different.

3. His beard looks awful. It is too long and has too many stray hairs. He really needs to _____ it so that it looks clean and taken care of.

4. I told the barber to _____ but look at this. He cut it way too short. I'm almost bald now because of him. I'm never going back to that shop again.

Activities

Beginning

1. Using the vocabulary from part two above (haircuts), create a dialogue with a partner about getting a haircut.
2. Go to a hairstylist store in the mall and observe the behaviors. What do you see? What is the same and/or different from your country? Write down any vocabulary you hear that you don't know or don't understand.

3. Go a department store and take pictures or make a list of all the hygiene products. Bring the list and/or pictures back to class. Classify them into their different purposes and if they are count or non-count nouns.

Intermediate

1. Prepare a presentation about the hygiene habits of people in your country. What's the same and what's different than the hygiene habits of Americans?

2. Analyze the conversation and compare it to a typical conversation in your country with a hairstylist/barber. How does Terri make Jon feel welcome and special (lines 1–3)? What does Jon say and how does he say it when Terri asks him what he'd like to have done with his hair today (lines 5–10)? Role-play getting a haircut or visiting a hairstylist. Use the vocabulary in reading #2. Are there other vocabulary items you need?

Advanced

1. Find articles about bathing habits in America like the links below about showering and hair washing habits. Read them and then discuss the benefits or dangers of frequent showering. Can you think of any other arguments?

   a) Showering article
      http://health.howstuffworks.com/skin-care/daily/tips/daily-shower-skin1.htm

   b) Hair washing article
      http://health.howstuffworks.com/skin-care/scalp-care/tips/how-often-wash-hair.htm

   c) Quit Bathing article:
      http://www.huffingtonpost.com/2015/03/30/what-happens-dont-bathe-video_n_6968700.html?ncid=txtlnkusaolp00000592

2. Interview other international students about hair care in the United States. Where do women go to get their hair done and where do men go? How do they feel about getting a haircut in the United States as opposed to their countries? Are there things that hairstylists do in their home countries that are not common here in the US?

Chapter 12

Baseball: "America's Favorite Pastime"

Anna Willson

© Suzanne Tucker/Shutterstock.com

Student Learning Objectives

By the end of this unit, students will be able to:

- ▶ Understand the importance of baseball in American culture.
- ▶ Describe the basic rules of baseball.
- ▶ Use some English idioms related to baseball.

Warm-Up Questions

1. What are some popular sports in your country?
2. Who are some famous athletes in your country?
3. What is your favorite sport?
4. Who plays sports in your country?
5. What do most sports have in common?
6. Who is your favorite athlete?

© Will Hughes/Shutterstock.com

READING 1

Vocabulary

Icon (n)	League (n)	Win it all (vp)
Love affair (np)	T-ball (n)	Regular season (np)
Little League (n)	Bat (n, v)	Playoffs (n)
Fan (n)	Color barrier (n)	World Series (n)
Team (n)	Retire (v)	Evoke (v)
Stick (n)	Time limit (np)	Nostalgia (n)
Softball (n)	Run (n)	Diverse (adj)
Segregate (v)	Unique (adj)	Establish (v)

The Boys of Summer

1   The first day of baseball comes in April every year and for many Americans marks the beginning of sum-
2   mer. Since the invention of baseball in the 1800s, Americans have been fascinated with the game and its
3   players. Baseball has become an important part of American culture. For example, most people know
4   who Babe Ruth, Mickey Mantle, and Jackie Robinson are. They are some of the **icons** of baseball. And
5   American English is full of expressions and idioms that come from America's favorite pastime.

© Suzanne Tucker/Shutterstock.com

6   The history of baseball in America begins before any other major organized sport. It is based on
7   similar games played in Europe during the 1700s. The first **teams** to play the game with rules similar to
8   today's rules were **established** in the middle of the 1800s in New York. The first professional baseball
9   leagues were formed in 1869. Two of the earliest teams, the Chicago White Stockings and the Boston Red
10 Caps are considered to be the oldest professional baseball teams in the country. Today these teams are
11 called the Chicago Cubs (White Stockings) and the Atlanta Braves (Boston Red Caps).

© Suzanne Tucker/Shutterstock.com

12   Our **love affair** with baseball often begins at an early age. Children often play baseball in the back-
13 yard or in an empty street with only a **stick** and a ball and articles of clothing to mark the bases. Com-
14 munities across the country have summer leagues for all ages. Very young children may play **T-ball**,
15 while older kids will play **Little League**. Adults will play **softball**. Many high schools and colleges have
16 baseball teams for boys and softball teams for women.

© Shaiith/Shutterstock.com

17   Baseball does not require a lot of equipment, just a **bat**, ball, and glove and place to play. It is also a
18   sport that anyone can play. Professional baseball teams are also very **diverse**. There are African Ameri-
19   can, White, Japanese, Korean, Dominican Republic, Cuban, and other players, making professional
20   American baseball a truly international sport.

21   Although all sports **fans** have strong feelings for their team and favorite players, baseball seems to
22   **evoke** more **nostalgia** than other sports. Almost everyone knows the story of Lou Gehrig, who suffered
23   from myotrophic lateral sclerosis (ALS), also known as Lou Gehrig's disease. He gave an unforgettable
24   farewell speech on the New York Yankees' field before he had to quit playing baseball for health reasons.
25   Even most non-athletic fans know of the famous Babe Ruth, who became a national hero for hitting 714
26   home runs, more than any other player at the time. Some people still consider the Sultan of Swat to be
27   the greatest baseball player ever.

28   Before 1947 baseball was **segregated**. There were the all-white Major **Leagues** and there was the
29   Negro League, which only had African American players. In 1947, Jackie Robinson became the first Afri-
30   can American to cross the **color barrier** and play for the all-white Brooklyn Dodgers. Jackie Robinson's
31   jersey number, 42 has been **retired** from all of professional baseball. No one on any team can ever wear
32   his number again. No other player in any sport has received this honor. Jackie Robinson died in 1972.

33   The rules of baseball also help make it popular. The most **unique** rule in baseball is that there is no
34   time. Most sports, such as basketball, football, soccer, and hockey, have a **time limit**. In football, for
35   example, the game is played for 60 minutes. In soccer, the game is played for 90 minutes. Yet, in baseball,
36   there is no time limit. This can potentially lead to very long games, especially if there is a tie (both teams
37   having the same number of runs), and the game continues until the tie is broken. The longest baseball
38   game ever played lasted 33 innings taking 2 days, 8 hours and 25 minutes. It also gives fans a feeling of
39   hope because the game is not over until the last out is made. Another thing unique about baseball is that
40   the defense controls the ball. In most other sports, the offense controls the ball as they try to score points,
41   but in baseball, the defense controls the ball, making it more difficult for the offense to score runs.

42   The Major League Baseball (MLB) season goes from April to October. At the beginning of every sea-
43   son, every team and its fans believe that this will be their year to **win it all**, the World Series. There are
44   two competing leagues, the National League and the American League. During the **regular season**, each
45   team plays 162 games. This is a lot compared to the NFL, which only has 16 games, and 82 games for the
46   NBA. After the regular season is over, there are the **playoffs** where only the best teams of the season play,
47   and then finally the **World Series** where the best team from the National League and the best team from
48   the American League compete for best overall team of the season.

49   Because of baseball's long history in the US, its accessibility, iconic players, and symbolic optimism,
50   baseball continues to be "America's favorite pastime."

Comprehension Questions

1. Why is America fascinated with baseball?
    a) Because it begins in April
    b) Because it is the oldest organized sport
    c) Because it has a long and rich history
    d) Because there is no time limit

2. According to the article, what are the oldest professional baseball teams in America?
    a) _____
    b) _____

3. Which of the following are <u>NOT</u> required to play baseball?
    a) Fans
    b) Glove
    c) Ball
    d) Bat

4. What does **diverse** in line 18 mean?
    a) Multiple
    b) Similar
    c) Ethnic
    d) Mixed

5. Who is the Sultan of Swat in line 26?
    a) Mickey Mantle
    b) Babe Ruth
    c) Jackie Robinson
    d) None of the above

6. Why did Major League baseball retire Jackie Robinson's number?
    a) To show respect for his contribution to baseball.
    b) Because he helped end segregation in baseball.
    c) Because he died in 1972.
    d) Both a and b

7. Which of the following make baseball unique from other sports?
    a) There are umpires.
    b) The defense is in control of the ball.
    c) There are no ties.
    d) There is no time limit.

8. If a team wins it all, what have they done?
    a) Won the regular season
    b) Won the playoffs
    c) Won the World Series
    d) All of the above

READING 2

© Eugene Onischenko/Shutterstock.com

Vocabulary

Objects	People	Actions	Events
Bat	Pitcher	Pitch	Strike out
Ball	Runner	Hit	Walk
Glove	Catcher	Catch	Home run
Bases (1st, 2nd 3rd)	Baseman (1st, 2nd, 3rd)	Slide	Foul
Home plate	Umpire	Steal	Fair
Infield	Manager	Bunt	Inning
Outfield	Fan	Swing	Run
Diamond	Batter	Strike	Ball
	Runner	Tag	Out

The Basics of Baseball

1 To understand the game of baseball, it's important to know the basic rules of play.
2 The basic object is to score more **runs** (points) than the other team. A baseball game has 9 **innings**
3 and each inning has 6 **outs**, 3 outs for each team. An inning is divided into two parts, the top half and
4 the bottom half. Each team plays on the defense and offense during an inning. When team A is playing
5 defense, they are in the field and control the ball. The objective for the defense (Team A) is to force Team
6 B (offense) to make 3 outs. Team B's objective is to try to **hit** the baseball away from the players on Team
7 A and for the runner to touch all 4 **bases** before Team A gets 3 outs.
8 Each team is made up of 9 players and a **manager**. In addition to the 9 players, there are **umpires**
9 who watch the game and decide if a player is out or safe, if a ball is **fair** or **foul**, and if a pitcher throws a
10 strike or a ball.
11 To make an out, Team A must (a) catch the ball in the air before it hits the ground, (b) throw the ball
12 to a base before a runner gets to the base, (c) **tag** the runner when he is not touching a base, or (d) strike
13 the batter out. A **strikeout** is when a batter swings at a ball and misses three times.

14   If Team B (the offense) hits the ball and no one catches it, the batter runs to the **first base**. Then Team
15   B tries to advance the **runner** on first base by hitting another ball safely away from Team A. This contin-
16   ues until the runner for Team B has touched first base, second base, third base, and finally **home plate**,
17   the fourth base. When a runner makes it to home plate safely, it is called a run.

© Flavio Beltran/Shutterstock.com

18   During an inning, the **pitcher** throws balls to the **catcher** who is sitting behind home plate. The
19   pitcher tries to throw balls past the batter without it being hit by the **batter**. If the pitcher throws 3 balls
20   past the batter, then the batter is out. If the pitcher throws a ball away from home plate, out of the strike
21   zone, it is called a ball. If the pitcher throws 4 balls, the batter is allowed to go to first base freely.
22   Once Team A has gotten 3 outs, the teams switch sides and Team B then goes on defense (to the field)
23   and Team A goes on offense (to bat). A game is over when one team has gotten a total of 27 outs against
24   the other team and the score is not tied. If the score is tied after 9 innings and 27 outs, the game goes into
25   extra innings and continues until the tie is broken.
26   The offense scores runs when a batter hits the ball safely away from the defense and runs to and
27   touches all four bases. If a batter hits the ball and runs to first base safely, that is called a single. If the bat-
28   ter hits a ball and runs to second base, it is called a double. A triple is when a batter hits the ball and runs
29   to third base safely. Finally, a **home run** is when the batter hits the ball out of the ballpark where no one
30   on the defense can catch it.

Comprehension Questions

1.   How many innings are there in a baseball game?
   a)   9
   b)   6
   c)   27
   d)   3

2.   How many bases are there in baseball?
   a)   1
   b)   2
   c)   3
   d)   4

3. A baseball game can end in a tie.
   a) True
   b) False

4. How can a player make an out? (Check all that apply)
   a) Hit a home run
   b) Catch the ball in the air before it hits the ground
   c) Tag a runner when he is not touching a base
   d) Swing and miss the ball three times

5. Who controls the ball?
   a) Defense
   b) Offense

6. What is a point called in baseball?
   a) Strike
   b) Hit
   c) Catch
   d) Run

7. When a batter hits the ball and runs to 2nd base, what is this called?
   a) A single
   b) A double
   c) A triple
   d) A home run

Baseball Fundamentals

1. Use pictures, video, or demonstrations to familiarize students with the basic vocabulary. More advanced students could also be introduced to additional vocabulary, such as *shortstop*, *balk*, *error*, *pinch hitter*, *seventh inning stretch*, *grand slam*, etc.

   The baseball field:

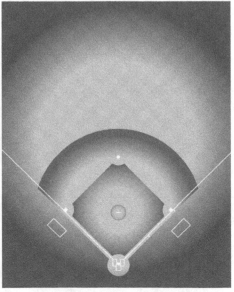

© enterlinedesign/Shutterstock.com

2.   Chose an inning of a taped baseball game to watch with the class, pointing out the players and the various actions, so that students will learn the sequence of play.

Baseball and English Idioms

A. Read the following dialogue with a partner. Guess the meaning of the underlined phrases from the context.

1	Pablo:	How did your presentation go today?
2	Yoko:	Well, I thought I'd <u>covered all the bases:</u> I had my note cards ready, I had proofread my
3		PowerPoint slides, and I practiced 10 times in front of a mirror.
4	Pablo:	So it went well?
5	Yoko:	No, I really <u>struck out</u>.
6	Pablo:	Oh, sorry. What went wrong?
7	Yoko:	Well, <u>right off the bat</u>, there was a problem with my computer files, and I couldn't get my
8		PowerPoint slides to open.
9	Pablo:	Oh, <u>strike one</u>…
10	Yoko:	Yeah, and then the professor <u>threw us a curve ball</u> and said we had to use five vocabulary
11		words from this week's list in our presentation. I was not prepared for that at all!
12	Pablo:	I hate it when that happens.
13	Yoko:	And then, my presentation was about the tea ceremony in Japan, but, <u>out of left field</u>, the other
14		students started asking me questions about coffee, and I didn't know how to answer them.
15		<u>Strike three</u>!
16	Pablo:	Well, we have another presentation next week. You'll just have <u>to step up to the plate</u> and give
17		it your best effort. Don't worry. I'm sure you'll <u>hit a home run</u> and get an A!

B. Match the baseball idioms to their meaning:

1. to cover all the bases
2. to strike out
3. right off the bat
4. to throw someone a curve
5. out of left field
6. strike three
7. to step up to the plate
8. to hit a home run

a. the last of a series of mistakes leading to failure
b. to take responsibility for a challenge
c. to fail
d. at the very beginning
e. to be prepared for any problem
f. to succeed
g. to make an unexpected request or requirement
h. in an unrelated or unanticipated way

C. Using the idioms in the dialogue or additional ones listed below, assign each student an idiom to look up and/or ask other Americans for the meaning. Students can present their findings in short class presentations, poster presentations, or class blog posts.

Other baseball-related idioms: **a ball park figure, in the ballpark, batting a thousand, play hardball, go to bat for someone, touch base, to have two strikes against you, on the ball, big league, minor league, on deck, pinch hitter, go down swinging, swing for the fences**

© cdrin/Shutterstock.com

Baseball and American Culture

A. Listen to any one of numerous versions of "Take Me Out to the Ballpark" on YouTube. Here are the lyrics for the frequently sung chorus:

> Take me out to the ball game,
> Take me out with the crowd;
> Just buy me some <u>peanuts</u> and <u>Cracker Jack</u>s,
> I don't care if I never get back.
> Let me root, root, root for the home team,
> If they don't win, it's a shame.
> For it's one, two, three strikes, you're out,
> At the old ball game.

B. Watch the movie "The Rookie" (2002, Rated G)

Questions for Discussion

1. Why did Jim give up his dream of playing professional baseball?
2. How does his dream motivate his students?
3. How does baseball affect Jim's relation with his father? Wife? Son?
4. What does Jim risk to become a professional player? Do you think he made a good decision?

C. Other baseball-themed movies:

1. 42 (2013) (History of Jackie Robinson)
2. Million Dollar Arm (2014) (Story about Indians playing Baseball)
3. The Natural (1984) (Robert Redford: Romantic Movie)
4. Field of Dreams (1989) (Kevin Costner: Romantic Movie)

5. Pride of the Yankees (1942) (History of Lou Gehrig)
6. Mr. 3000 (2004) (Comedy)
7. A League of their Own (1992) (History of Women's Baseball)
8. 61* (2001) (History of the most home runs in a single season)
9. For the Love of the Game (1999) (Kevin Costner: Romantic—No Hitter)
10. Eight Men Out (1988) (History of Chicago White Sox who gambled on the World Series)
11. Mr. Baseball (Tom Selleck goes to play baseball in Japan)

D. For more information, check out these websites:

   1. MLB.com (the official website of Major League Baseball)
   2. http://www.pbs.org/search/?q=baseball
   3. http://www.ncaa.com/sports/baseball/d1
   4. http://baseballhall.org/ (the official Baseball Hall of Fame website)
   5. http://www.littleleague.org

E. For a very advanced class, find a copy of Abbot and Costello's famous vaudeville act, "Who's on First" on YouTube. This could be a fun way to learn more about the game, what it means to American culture, and to analyze how words are used in this comic act.

F. There are 30 professional MLB teams in the US. This could be turned into a US geography lesson. Have students research the cities where a baseball team is located: What is there to do in these cities? What are the good restaurants? What schools, universities, or government offices are there? What is the cost of living? What is the weather like in these cities, etc., and then have students give a presentation on what they learned.

G. Contact the community relations department of a local university to arrange a visit from student athletes. Many welcome the opportunity to fulfill community service opportunities.

H. Arrange for students to attend a university baseball or softball game. For slightly more money, a pro or minor league game may also be available.

I. During the offseason, students may enjoy touring a stadium or watching a team practice.

J. Even in a small area, baseball can be played with a spongy ball (Nerf) or wiffle ball and bat. Playing sports with students is an excellent way to build rapport and classroom teamwork. Another game that can be played to simulate baseball is kickball and does not require lots of extra equipment. https://en.wikipedia.org/wiki/Kickball

Chapter 13

Snowed Under

Michael Schwartz

© Vadym Zaitsev/Shutterstock.com

Student Learning Objectives

By the end of this unit, students will be able to:

► Talk about different weather conditions, specifically winter weather conditions.
► Use vocabulary specific to winter weather.
► Understand a weather report.
► Have survival strategies for winter weather.

Discussion Questions

With a partner, discuss the questions below.

1. What is your favorite season?
2. How many seasons do you have in your country?
3. What is "winter" like in your country?
4. What are the different kinds of storms in your country?
5. What do you do to protect yourself from these storms?
6. How would you describe "snow" to someone who has never seen it before?
7. What is the weather like where you are right now?
8. What do you think the title means? Can the idiom be used to describe other situations besides the weather? Do you have a similar expression in your language?

© Konstanttin /Shutterstock.com

READING 1

Vocabulary

Wind chill (n)
Temperature (n)
Freezing (adj)
Blizzard (n)
Fahrenheit (n)
Celsius (n)
Put on (v)

Bundle up (v)
Ice over (v)
Drop (v)
Below freezing (np)
Frostbite (n)
Strike up (v)
Break the ice (idiom)

Climate (n)
Deal with (v)
Ups and downs (idiom)
Survival kit (n)
Help (n)
Whiteout (n)

Winter

1   Weather is not controlled by humans like other cultural behaviors. But it is something that people have
2 to adjust to when they go to another country. In some countries, it may be hot all the time. In other coun-
3 tries it may be cold most of the time. While in other countries, there may be four distinct seasons, winter,
4 spring, summer, and autumn or fall.

© Madlen/Shutterstock.com   © sianc/Shutterstock.com

5   Weather is also something that people like to talk about. If you want to **strike up** a conversation with
6 someone, talking about the weather is a good way to **break the ice**. Why? This is because weather is a
7 safe topic to talk about. Other topics like money and politics are not common subjects that Americans
8 talk about freely with strangers. Weather, however, is something we all have to **deal with** and everyone
9 has an opinion about the weather. Some people like cold, snowy weather while others hate it and prefer
10 warmer or hot weather. Some people like rain while others prefer dry **climates**.

11   All seasons have their **ups and downs**, or good things and bad things. It's good to know about these
12 things, especially the bad things so you can prepare for the season and protect yourself.

13   Winter can be a wonderful season. There are many exciting and fun activities that people do during
14 winter, like snow skiing, snow boarding, sledding, snow shoeing, ice skating, and even making a snow-
15 man. If you **bundle up** with warm clothes, like hats, scarves, gloves, warm shoes, and coats, then you can
16 find a lot of fun things to do in winter. Snow is also beautiful. When snow falls, it sometimes comes down
17 softly and gently. It covers everything: trees, roads, houses, and the ground. It often looks like a white
18 blanket, making everything look clean and pure.

19   During the winter, it is important to pay attention to the weather. Most smartphones and tablets
20 today have weather apps. These apps can give temperature readings in both **Fahrenheit** and **Celsius**.
21 When it begins to get really cold, people will talk about **wind chill**. Wind chill is not the same as air tem-
22 perature. Air temperature is what you can see on your weather app, but wind chill is what it really feels
23 like outside. For example, the air temperature might be 30°F, but if the wind is strong, the real tempera-
24 ture might be 15°F. It's important to know what the wind chill temperature is during winter.

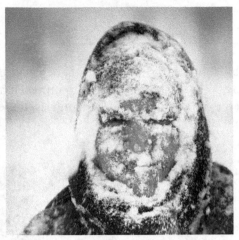

© Jan Mika/Shutterstock.com

25   Winter can also be dangerous if you are not prepared for it. For example, when the temperature
26 **drops** to –25°F, **frostbite** can set in very quickly. At –25° a person's skin will begin to freeze in less than
27 30 minutes. If a person gets severe frostbite they might lose an arm, hand, leg, foot, or worse.
28   **Blizzards** are another concern in winter. Blizzards are big snowstorms along with high winds. The
29 strong winds and snow will create a **whiteout**, making it difficult to see to drive or even walk. People
30 caught in a blizzard can easily get lost outside because they cannot see what's around them. If you are
31 driving and get caught in a blizzard, it is best to stay in your car until **help** arrives. If you do have to get
32 out of your car, then it is a good idea to tie a rope around you and attach it to the car so that you can find
33 your way back to the car when you need to.

© Benoit Daoust/Shutterstock.com

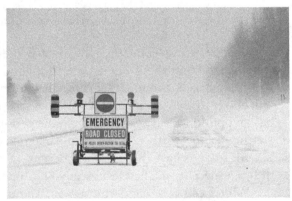

© Phil McDonald/Shutterstock.com

34   Finally driving in winter when there is snow on the ground can be dangerous. The roads may be **iced**
35 **over**. When the roads are covered with ice, driving is difficult because the car cannot be controlled as
36 easily as when the roads are dry. It is always wise to have a **survival kit** in your car during the winter. A
37 survival kit should include a blanket, water, high-energy food, a flashlight, shovel, windshield scraper,
38 and candle.

© Stuart Monk/Shutterstock.com

39   It may sound like winter is no fun and that people should live where there isn't snow and freezing
40   rain and sub-zero temperatures, but that is not true. Winter can be the best season of the year. As long
41   as you are prepared and pay attention to the local weather forecast, you can find many wonderful things
42   to do in winter.

Comprehension Questions

1. Why do people like to talk about the weather?
    a) It affects everyone.
    b) It is dangerous.
    c) It is something that humans cannot control.
    d) It changes every season.

2. Which word or phrase below is a synonym for **break the ice** as it is used in line 6?
    a) Hard
    b) Split
    c) Start
    d) Shatter

3. Which of the following clothes would you not likely wear in the winter?
    a) Gloves
    b) Scarf
    c) Coat
    d) Sandals

4. What is wind chill (line 21)?
    a) The real temperature.
    b) The temperature of the wind.
    c) A weather app on smartphones and tablets.
    d) The air temperature.

5. What can happen if the temperature is –20°F outside?
    a) You can have a blizzard.
    b) You can get frostbite very quickly.
    c) You can get lost.
    d) You can see water freeze.

6. Which of the following should you keep in your car during the winter?
    a) Shovel
    b) Blanket
    c) Food and water
    d) All of the above

Vocabulary

Match the words in the left-hand column with the correct synonym or definition in the right-hand column.

1.	Bundle up	A.	Environment
2.	Ups and downs	B.	Put on lots of warm clothes
3.	Whiteout	C.	Manage
4.	Strike up	D.	To be covered with ice
5.	Ice over	E.	Begin a conversation
6.	Below freezing	F.	Temperature under 32°F or 0°C
7.	Drop	G.	Blizzard or blowing snow
8.	Deal with	H.	Good things and bad things
		I.	To go down

READING 2

Vocabulary

Man (adv)	Temps (n)	For sure (pp)
Weatherman	So ready (adv)	Have a good one (vp)
Blew (v)	Fire up (vp)	I'd say
Brutal (adj)	Soak up (vp)	can't wait
Get a break (vp)	Brave the cold (vp)	degree (°)

© connel/Shutterstock.com

Dialogue

1	Bus driver:	That'll be $1.50 exact change only.
2	Man:	Here you go. Thanks. Excuse me is anyone sitting here? (sits next to woman)
3	Woman:	No
4	Man:	Man is it cold out there.
5	Woman:	Yeah it is.
6	Man:	The **weatherman** said it would be warmer today.
7	Woman:	It was 10° when I left the house today.
8	Man:	I know, but I thought it was supposed to be 30° today.
9	Woman:	Yeah, well it looks like they **blew** the forecast.
10	Man:	I'd say.
11	Woman:	I'm **so ready** for spring.
12	Man:	Me too. I like winter but this one has gone on too long.
13	Woman:	It's been a **brutal** one this year, that's for sure.
14	Man:	I've heard we might **get a break** sometime next week and that the **temps** are going to get to
15		about 40°.
16	Woman:	That would be nice. I'm tired of having to bundle up every morning to go to work. I'm
17		ready for some nice spring weather.
18	Man:	Yeah, I'd like to get out play some golf, **fire up** the grill, and just **soak up** some rays.
19	Woman:	I can't wait to see spring flowers and robins.
20	Man:	I hear ya. Well, time to go **brave the cold**.
21	Woman:	**Have a good one**.
22	Man:	You too.

Comprehension Questions

1. Where are the man and woman?
    a) At school
    b) In a taxi
    c) At home
    d) On a bus

2. What is the relationship between the man and woman?
    a) Husband and wife
    b) Strangers
    c) Classmates
    d) Friends

3. What does the word *blew* mean as it is used in line 9?
    a) It's windy outside.
    b) The weatherman's prediction was wrong.
    c) It's very cold outside.
    d) The weatherman's prediction was perfect.

4. Which of the following is closest in meaning to **I'd say** in line 10?
    a) I want to talk.
    b) I want tell you something.
    c) I disagree.
    d) I agree.

5. What does the man mean in line 14 when he says **get a break**?
    a) Take a vacation from the cold.
    b) Have some relief from the cold.
    c) Break the ice.
    d) Relax from the cold temperatures.

6. What does the man want to do when spring comes in line 18?
    a) Have a barbeque
    b) Sit in the sun
    c) Play golf
    d) All of the above

7. What does **can't wait** mean in line 19?
    a) Flowers and robins are signs of spring.
    b) To like pretty things.
    c) To be excited about something in the future.
    d) The woman is impatient.

8. What does go **brave the cold** mean in line 20?
    a) To be courageous to go outside where it's cold.
    b) To go outside where it's cold.
    c) To leave.
    d) To be crazy to go outside in the cold.

9. What's another way to say *have a good one* as in line 21?
    a) Hope you are well.
    b) See you again.
    c) Good-bye.
    d) Have a good day.

Winter-Related Idioms

Break the ice	Freeze our butts off	Snowball effect
Under the weather	Come in from the cold	Cold snap
Put on ice	Leave out in the cold	Hibernate
Snowed under/in	Cold shoulder	Snowbound
Fair-weather friend	On thin ice	A snowball's chance in hell

Activities

Beginning

1. Have students create role-play conversations where they talk about the weather using vocabulary, expressions, and idioms from this unit.
2. Have students create and film their own weather report.
3. If there's fresh snow on the ground, go outside and make a snowman and snow angel.
4. Go to the following NOAA website for more information about winter weather preparedness and using this information along with other information, create a public service announcement (PSA). Post this PSA on YouTube or your IEP's facebook page.

   ○ Weather survival kit: National Oceanic and Atmospheric Administration: http://www.nws.noaa.gov/om/winter/before.shtml

Intermediate

1. Watch or listen to a weather report and analyze it for its organization. What comes first, what's second, etc. What's the most important part of the weather report?
2. Read *To Build a Fire* by Jack London or watch the movie: https://www.youtube.com/watch?v=RBB06RLmCcU

   ○ Stop the movie 15 minutes before it ends and have students predict the ending and then write their own ending. This could be turned into a short skit.

Advanced

1. Have students research weather related phenomena such as SAD (Seasonal Affective Disorder), global warming, the jet stream, the flu season, winter sports or activities, etc.
2. Students can create a survey to find out what people like about winter, what they do in the winter, and what they don't like about winter.
3. Have students investigate the origins and meanings of the idioms in the table above using Urban Dictionary http://www.urbandictionary.com or another website.

CPSIA information can be obtained
at www.ICGtesting.com
Printed in the USA
LVHW050807190820
663469LV00002B/6